Design for Effective Selling Space

JOSEPH WEISHAR

McGraw-Hill, Inc.

New York	Hamburg	Oklahoma City
St. Louis	Lisbon	Paris
San Francisco	London	San Juan
	Madrid	Sãn Paulo
Aukland	Mexico City	Singapore
Bogotá	Milan	Sydney
Caracas	Montreal	Tokyo
	New Delhi	Toronto

Weishar, Joseph.
    Design for effective selling space / by Joseph Weishar
       p.   cm.
    Includes bibliographical references and index.
    ISBN 0-07-069110-X
    1. Stores decoration--Psychological aspects. 2. Interior
architecture. 3. Consumer behavior. I. Title.
NK2195.S89W45   1992
725',21--dc20

                                            91-44954
                                             CIP

1234567890 HAL/HAL   9765432

ISBN 0-07-069110-X

The editors for this book were Joel Stein and Vilma Barr, and the design was
by Carrie Berman Design. Editorial and design coordination was by Business &
Professional Editorial Services, Inc. This book was set in Bodoni Book,
Helvetica, and Zurich. It was created electronically by Carrie Berman Design
using Quark® 3.0 on the Apple® Macintosh™.

Printed and bound by Arcata Graphics/Halliday.

For more information about other McGraw-Hill materials, call
1-800-2-MCGRAW in the United States. In other countries, call your nearest
McGraw-Hill office.

Table of Contents

Dedicated to those pragmatic/romantic
dreamers who are determined to make their
New Vision a reality.

To Margo and Peter, for sharing the joy in
their accomplishments and lives.

And to my mother, Jessie, whose glow
penetrates all who touch her.

Introduction

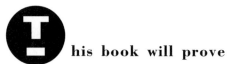his book will prove that store design and merchandise presentation influence customer behavior. Through an understanding of sensory triggering mechanisms, seemingly random and chaotic customer patterns will have predetermined responses. The sensitivities of people in a controlled environment cause repetitive actions that are codified in this book. Their use sets a logical sequence in establishing selling space priorities.

The causes of this predictable behavior can be incorporated into a designed imagery system. The competitive edge derived from the use of this information will generate initial and continuing higher levels of productivity, for both the retail selling space and the store's staff.

The point-of-sale generates more sales than the combined percentages of all media. The job of designers and merchants is to set the merchandise in a selling space so that it can be seen, serviced, and purchased in the easiest way possible. When this happens, customers stay longer, buy more, and have a good time doing it. An environment that is conducive to shopping must take into account all the physical and psychological effects that initiate and motivate customer activity.

A LASTING IMAGE

No two shops are alike. The way they look reflects the image of the company's current stated mission, as interpreted by all of its employees. The contribution to the presentation by all participants in a retail enterprise must be seen as logical to any prospective customer. Successful stores correctly interpret human potential in the space of their store.

The customer's first impression of the store's environment is the most lasting. It is created by a balance of all the elements of the store's design and presentation of the merchandise.

Designers who use market information to plan a store for their retail client must also use the classical, traditional, historical, repetitive actions of customers in a market place.

Designers and merchants can, to an astonishing degree, obtain specific desired results from customers *by understanding what those customers expect, and then giving them more than their expectations.* The pieces that form those expectations are the keys to entice targeted customers. The essential actions of the customers–first as people, and then as a shoppers– provide the basis for continuing this enticement inside the store.

Retailers and designers must learn to correctly interpret and verbalize the response of the customer. There is a vocabulary that can be used to properly express the actions and reactions of all shoppers. The transfer of that information allows the staff to set the department to take advantage of the natural shopping tendencies of the store's customers.

Only four percent of all customers will inform the store of a poor shopping experience. This makes it all the more important for store owners and designers to comprehend customers' actions. Design can account for the creation of possibilities that will permit the maximum potential of the operation. In fact, the design and designer form a conduit, or a bridge, that visually and physically translates historical market and sales data into a functional, practical, aesthetically pleasing shop. Although there are many ways to use hard facts to support any argument for design, it is still the creative designers and merchants, the intuitive synthesizers, who elevate the essence of the idea into a unique, memorable, rewarding shopping experience.

We will examine customer motives and actions. At the same time, we will get more insight into ourselves. Judgment of the action of others stems from a self-realization of our own propensities. *We are all, at one time or another, shoppers.* With that in mind, we should be able to initially trust and use our own reactions to the many suggestions and tests that are incorporated in the following pages. If customers are predictable, then so are we all. An examination and exploration of the ideas in this book will help us strip away the prejudices that separate the seller and the buyer, or the designer and the merchant.

Chapter One

Factors That Influence Customers

BEFORE THEY ENTER A STORE

ustomers develop opinions of a store even before they enter. They are able to form these opinions prior to entry from the many signals that are sent by store management. Before customers leave for a shopping trip, images are formed that establish their level of expectation which the store should meet, or exceed. A planned program of out-of-store communications by management maintains the consistency of image from first perceptions through to the sale and the checkout. *Retailers can communicate concretely with their customers by visual images.* When we examine common traits of the images sent, and codify them, they form an understanding of customer decision-making while they shop.

There are eight ways that customers form an opinion of what they will find inside the store. Some of these are directly under the control of the retailer. Other opinions are formed as a secondary result of those efforts

- *Advertising: all media*
- *Location*
- *Exterior design*
- *Signs: logo and name*
- *Word-of-mouth*
- *Previous visits*
- *Approach: by car, on foot*
- *Display Windows*

(1.1)

A and B: Bloomingdale's, New York City. The catalogue photo was taken at the same time that this bedding presentation was shown on the sales floor. Inconsistency in visual presentation hurts sales by altering expectations.

ADVERTISING - PRINT MEDIA

Most stores use catalogs, direct mail, newspaper, and magazine advertising. Retail print media demonstrates a high level of graphic presentation. The graphic design, photography, printing, paper, and clarity are often superb. In fact, catalog art has recently set the pace in retail graphic design.

But, unhappily, some stores who issue these handsome catalogs and fine ads do *not* reflect the same quality once the customers are inside the doors. On the other hand, there are some fine stores whose catalog presentation is not representative of the superb presentation of merchandise in the department. Photo catalogs of mass retailers, just as their merchandise selection, and the environment in which they are presented, must reflect better value on a measurable price scale.

ADVERTISING - ELECTRONIC MEDIA

Radio and TV broadcast a store's intended quality. Radio ads travel with the customer from home or office. Voice association produces images from sultry to ethnic. Because there is no visual image on radio to hint at what the customer will see in the store, the imagination is set free to make associated pictures.

The removal, by law, of cigarette advertising from TV opened up large blocks of air time. With these costly gaps posing a serious threat to income, the stations sought potential advertisers who could cover this loss by absorbing large chunks of time. In the first wave of excitement about cost per viewer, compared with other media, retailers jumped in whole-heartedly, and prematurely. Although the networks and the local stations gave all the technical advice, and ad agencies set up retail divisions, the media picture did not consistently project the intended image of the point-of-sale.

Few retailers could use the clout of a national network, or even take all the advertising time for a full half-hour. The initial mix between the institutional, promotional, and sale advertising did not dovetail with other more conventional print ads. The quality of the retailers TV ads were not equal to the TV ads placed by national advertisers who had many years of prior marketing experience. In newspaper advertising, where stores had a history of acceptance and expertise, the difference was not noticeable, but on TV the comparison hurt.

By a stroke of fortunate timing, Lord & Taylor had, during the time of the newspaper strike of 1962-63, pre-pared a series of wispy women's clothing TV commercials that were produced by the in-house staff. Not only did they get consumer notice, but they told a beautifully clear fashion story that sold merchandise and added to the lustre of the newly-renovated store.

The extension of TV advertising by direct sales via cable with telephone or computer linkage in the home was a natural off-shoot. So far, the jury is out on its effectiveness. The entertainment aspect of the shopping experience may be lost in the media translation. The effect on the bottom line thus far has not been cost efficient.

Instances abound where development dollars have been abandoned because of poor results. For ATT, IBM, Sears, J.C. Penney, American Express and others, the poor response to purchasing merchandise at home has been too great to sustain a large-scale continuing effort.

Yet, somone, someday, will figure out the proper balance between merchandise, marketing, delivery and entertainment to dwarf current out-of-store sales.

Successful retailers use advertising to encourage shoppers to enter the store where they see the 95% or more balance of the store's offering.

(1.2)

Burlington Arcade, London. The lovely architecture binds all stores in this mall into one aesthetic ethic to the benefit of all.

LOCATION

The location of the store will give the customer a specific idea of the level of expected quality. Whether the store is in center city, in a regional mall, or a freestanding pad store (a store that is not attached to another store or a mall) the geographic location sets an image. Location as a convenience is important, but convenience shopping alone is not the major criteria for the success of a store. In enclosed malls, both the location and the name of the mall are image makers. *Shoppers usually recall the name of a mall before they think of the name of the store.*

Stores in strip malls, however, have retained their identification. The architecture of a strip mall that permits the store name on the facade puts the emphasis on the projection of personality of the tenants.

EXTERIOR DESIGN

The *architecture* of malls has neutralized individual store architecture. Even when successful stores are clustered in spaces as beautiful and as striking as the Galeria Vittorio Emanuele II in Milan, or London's Burlington Arcade, few shoppers will remember an individual store facade.

Center city shops and large stores can be classified by the age and style of the structure. As customers approach a store, its architecture against the surrounding environment is a powerful first impression. The early entrepreneurs who oversaw the growth of their businesses knew this, and the theatrical emporium came of age. It was the early merchants who first established department stores, such as those who built on the "Ladies Mile" on lower Sixth Avenue in New York City. It was their desire to create a structure that could fulfill their dreams, as well as those of their clients. They made the building part of their total image.

LOGO AND SIGNS

Now, in place of memorable store facades in the inner city, the exterior image of stores in shopping centers is communicated primarily by the name and the design of the logo. The sign

and occasionally the facade have replaced the building as the exterior signature. The choices of signs and designs include script, block letters, back-lit, neon, pictorial, metal, wood, plastics, size and configuration.

Some city stores have no significant signs except for plaques at the entry or incised letters above the portal, and let the building itself determine the communicated image. It is almost axiomatic that the smaller the sign, the more exclusive and higher priced the merchandise. Most city department stores have their names on marquees or in large illuminated letters on the facade. Free-standing stores, including supermarkets, use a logo or a graphic and name combination. Each variation creates a different perception of price.

(1.3)

These store fronts represent the attitude, price perception, value, and target market by the combination of architecture, location, and signing.

(1.4)

Lord & Taylor, New York City. The action of customers moving in and out of a store, as well as the dress of those shoppers, helps to condition an entering shopper to the store's merchandise.

WORD OF MOUTH

Word-of-mouth is the most powerful promotional tool, because it carries the weight of respected friends and family. A shopper may tell three friends about a pleasant shopping experience. When on the other hand, the experience is less than anticipated, or poor, the chances are that a dozen friends would be informed. Worse yet, only four percent of all customers who have a complaint about the quality of the store will tell the management. The rest will consider shopping in other stores and take their business elsewhere.

PREVIOUS VISITS

Previous visits of the shopper are the best image of the store that the customer has. Here, shoppers have their own picture of what they saw, felt, heard, and smelled. They then modify their sensory experiences to make them more pleasant. They recall a sense of well-being and shopping astuteness that comes from making a smart purchase on prior trips.

APPROACH

As customers approach the store, even before they see merchandise in the windows, they become aware of autos in the parking spots on the street or mall parking areas, as well as other customers moving to and from the entry. Hardware stores with Mercedes convertibles in their parking lot signify a certain high degree of service, product, and price.

On the other hand, do not be too quick to judge the quality of shoppers driving lesser-priced autos or four-wheel drives. Sometimes these autos have a reverse snob appeal. The VW of 30 years ago had the same appeal to the yuppies of that generation.

The clothing and carriage of fellow shoppers tells more specific stories. The way that shoppers are groomed will generally present an impression that relates to economic status. Even when denims are worn, a sharp observer can pick out grooming and style differences.

Observing other shoppers does influence customers in areas such as exclusivity, price expectation, and current style availability.

WINDOWS

The last piece of information communicated to the shopper before entry is the windows. Here, the balance of the final prejudged expectation is made. The immediacy before entering carries the most weight in the shopper's mind.

Windows, even when representing a sale, must have an overall consistency with the quality of the product and the presentation. Over-selling a store at this final point by having windows that far outshine what is found inside can be the ultimate shopping disappointment.

When Alexander's opened its 59th Street and Lexington Avenue location in New York City, they started a tradition of superb imaginative windows that depended more on creativity than on cost. It matched the quality of

(1.5)

Bernard Perris, Madison Avenue, New York City. The photo and the subtlety of the pant cuff wrap is a distinct European touch in presentation.

merchandising and ambiance of the entire interior. The windows were so refreshing that comparisons were soon made to the windows of the store on the next street, Bloomingdale's. "Which is the fashion store?" the customers wanted to know. Bloomingdale's windows at that time were either conservative or simply unimaginative.

Very shortly after the arrival of Alexander's, a new visual team was brought into Bloomingdales that was headed by a trained scenic designer. The effect was electrifying and the balance between the two stores was corrected. The emphasis in Bloomingdale's shifted from standard charm to "merchandise first" with authority. Several visual merchandisers later made their reputations on the clever, appropriate, fashionable acceptance of Bloomingdale's by projecting an upbeat image through the the stores windows.

These examples of perception through communication demonstrate how customers start to form an impression of the store before they go inside. Even more powerful is the control that the retailer has over the customer's decision-making once they are in the store itself.

Chapters 2, 3 and 4 discuss factors that influence a customer's buying decision based on their psyche and physiology. A program of out-of-store communications combined with a use of the information contained in this book maintains a consistency of desired image from first perception outside the store, through to the sale, and the checkout in the store.

WEEK 4

Think Vs. See

Retail designers plan and merchandise a store in order to entice a customer to buy. Many times the intent of the designer is different from, if not opposite to, the reaction of the customer.

The previous chapter gave examples of how the expectation level of the customer is established outside the store. Once inside, customers receive a new set of images that adds to the perception of the store formed prior to entering. When the customer moves towards the merchandise area, impressions of price, quality and exclusivity that were intuitively percieved and formed are now confirmed.

Designers and retailers use architecture, fixtures, signs, and merchandise working together to sculpt the space. Customers should quickly and correctly interpret the intent of these visual features.

In the following examples, we will see how the intended message communicated to the customer is received and interpreted. These examples are selected from field observations and have been verified at the one point where customers "vote" - the sales register.

CUBIC SPACE

When customers see a spacious department, they automatically think higher prices and exclusivity, as well as professional sales service. Bergdorf Goodman has less merchandise per cubic foot than any large specialty store in New York. But the visual balance is matched by the result. Bergdorf Goodman reports one of the highest sales per square foot in the country, ranging between $1,000 and $2,000 per square foot.

AISLE WIDTH

In a Nouvelle Galeries store in Rouen, France, the women's department was remerchandised. The area was physically refreshed with paint and lighting. New mannequins were brought in to show more styles. Though the merchandise was exactly the same, and everyone agreed it looked better than before, sales dropped. To correct the situation the

department was observed and evaluated for several weeks. Maintenance was superb and there were more people browsing in the department but, fewer purchases.

The sales staff, buyers and central management could not make sense out of the situation, because they knew that they had created a better, and more serviceable department. Finally, the marketing director surveyed the customers. The results from the answers were virtually unanimous. The customers:

- *Liked the space more.*
- *Thought that the merchandise was different than before.*
- *Thought that the merchandise was more expensive.*

Bergdorf Goodman, New York City. Each area of the fashion floor was designed to have a home-like atmosphere. The merchandise is an indication of the styles available, and the customer expects, and receives, sales service.

Nouvelle Galeries, France. The interior department aisles were made to clarify the assortment. This photo shows the later changes when more merchandise was added.

(2.3)

Suzy Shier, Montreal. The fun presentation of printed sweatshirts is at the front of a specialty store. Visual messages become clear; the staff is style conscious and will give personal service.

In fact it was the same stock at the same price. In re-examining the remerchandising, it was found that the stock on the floor was better clustered, and the wall presentation held more items shown more clearly. This permitted wider internal aisles.

The customers equated these wider aisles with higher prices. Even though the price tickets never changed, the customers felt that they were in a higher priced department. *This seeming grand passage was where intent and interpretation were opposite.*

The buyers were then alerted and brought in more stock, rather than downsizing the department. Stock levels were corrected and sales increased when the balance of space, to merchandise groups, to aisle space, was adjusted.

WALL HEIGHT

Some stores create an atmosphere of junior departments by placing merchandise high on the wall. In a specialty store or a department store the image is the same. A youthful and playful effect is created. However, once a customer enters and sees merchandise that is displayed in three or more tiers, *they automatically believe that they will get sales-service, at least to retrieve the merchandise for examination.*

ITEM MULTIPLES

When merchandise is set on the floor, the quantity displayed for sale takes on a meaning of its own. Multiple presentation affects the perception of credibility, exclusivity, product desirability, scarcity, and price. Multiples in different surroundings assume a different meaning. Various environments in a discount store, a warehouse club, a department store, a specialty store, a category killer, a supermarket or a hypermarche also have a direct effect on the merchandise level acceptable to a customer. The same merchandise in each of these selling spaces demands a different unit quantity.

If merchandise in stackable containers has a recognizable national brand name, the product is treated as a commodity by the customer, and may gain credibility through multiple exposure. Even cosmetics and fragrances are judged in this manner. Other than counter cases, where sales-service is necessary, the merchandise must have a few physical presentation properties in order to seem credible and desirable to the customer. Whether the multiple packages are stacked on the floor or placed on shelves:

- *They must be reachable without bending.*
- *They should be eye level.*

Within those two criteria, many visual formats can account for increased sales. If the product sells well, the stock level drops. Usually products that are shown in multiples are replaceable. If they are not replaced at about the same speed as the rate of sale, the physical presence or "critical mass" on the floor is lessened and the sales drop. *Physically, when the stock is reduced and shoppers must lower their sight line to see the items, their perceptions of price and product desirability drops with it.* If no replacement items are available, dummy boxes, cubes, or tables will serve for a while.

The situation is quite different with RTW. Large quantities of the same items exposed at the same time, generally on the same fixture, are

almost always devalued in the customer's eye. The single exception to this occurs when customer traffic is so intense, that the herd instinct takes precedence, and urgency to buy overcomes factors of exclusivity. Even at Christmas, when stores have more shoppers, it is difficult for customers to justify a multiple exposure of the same item when the store is not consistently highly trafficked.

(2.4)

The use of the manufacturer's boxes reinforces a name that customers think of before they may think of the product. The bulk presentation permits the merchants to use the items in a multiple, diagonal manner.

The problems with this presentation are caused by a lack of understanding of what is going through the customer's mind. The low (physical height) level translates to the customer as either insufficient initial purchases, or a product that will not be replaced.

Other times, it is advisable to keep only two to three items of the same size, same color, and same style on a rack at one time. This system has several benefits:

- *The style will probably remain in stock through the shopping day.*
- *With about 12 pieces of the same SKU, it is easier for the staff to see stock movement. If six of one hundred pieces sell, virtually no movement can be seen. But, if six items sold out of twelve, out of stock situations can be noticed in inventory levels, and quickly acted on.*

2.5

There is no indication on this fixture that the merchandise is for sale or at a price point that justifies the quantity. Even if it does happen to sell, broken size ranges will not be noticed.

- *The price must justify the bulk. This occurs when the customer knows the general range of prices of a basic garment, or the range of prices in a designer/manufacturer label category. In bulk presentation the customer either finds the product undesirable, or will wait for a return visit to get the garment on clearance or mark-down. Whenever possible, it is better to feed the rack, rather than put all the merchandise out at once.*

LIGHTING

The myriad of illumination instruments and the sophistication of newly-marketed lamps have created enormous options for the retail designer. However, the resulting effects on the customer are virtually unchanged. The two issues in illumination that most affect a customer's perception are *intensity and light color*. The balance of those two are a major part of the whole impression given when all stimuli effects are measured.

If retail presentation is akin to theater, then it is lighting that can create that dramatic and lasting impression. Store lighting should help to direct the eye, as theatrical lighting does. In the theater the designer focuses the action of the moment, by spotlights, within an ambiance that is set for the total scene. *Space in a retail store should be sculpted with light, shaping the environment with intensity levels and color* (see Chapter 14).

Too often, however, track lighting positions that permit dramatic directional angles to light the merchandise as the stars in stores and in windows are not used, or worse, not considered.

The entire perimeter of the store is a position that can be used for side and back lighting as well as washing the wall with patterns and colors. A track that follows the perimeter is a place where lighting innovations may start. In windows, especially in many mall stores, the light track is not placed at the front edge of the window. This causes a problem, because the merchandise is then top lit or back lit. The change of presentations in a window necessitates the full range of spotlight positions–front, side, top, back, and footlighting. Plugging outlets are also recommended for electrical equipment, such as fans or turntables. These outlets are also used frequently by the visual merchandising crew when setting the merchandise in the window.

2.6

Tristan, Montreal. The combination of fluorescent, neon, incandescent, and quartz give this specialty store the ability to have high levels of ambient light and to spotlight the mannequins and merchandise at the same time. It indicates fashion at a price in the mind of the shopper.

(2.7)

**Clothes Tree, Knoxville, Tennessee.
This store incorporated a deep
mirrored valance around the interior
perimeter. When the panels were
removed, it exposed a light track that
added to the drama of the shop as
well as the merchandise presentation.
Also note that there are track lights
interspersed in the fluorescents. The
balance between the two types of
illumination was changed to reflect
sale periods and new fashion periods.**

Many retail designers use valance
lighting for ready-to-wear on the
walls. Light projected by almost all
valance lighting creates several nega-
tives.

- *The highest intensity illumination
  of the merchandise is on the
  shoulders, and not on the face or
  length of the garment. This happens because the valance depth,
  normally about 24" from the
  wall, mounts a fixture that only
  lights the top of the garment.*

- *Most valances also permit light to
  splash the wall above, moving the
  eye further away from the stock.*

- *If maintenance is not superb, it is
  likely that different fluorescents
  with different colors ratings are
  used. They create color variations
  when projected on the merchandise, but are more obvious on the
  wall above.*

(2.8)

**Even though the
merchandise can be
seen, the blast of
light on the wall
above and below the
valance wins the
fight for attention.**

NICHES

Feature presentation niches are architecturally designed and positioned. They are equipped with spotlights, and are in themselves a fairly good concept that forces a dramatic presentation of feature items. Most stores have few possibilities of adjusting niche size, and definitely not the location. This does not take into account the talent of store staff to make appealing presentations in an open space that is equipped with a reasonable lighting system. There is always a need to change the proportion of space used for new presentations. Differences in inventory levels, fabric density, and assortment width are not constants. They are best handled by a skilled merchandising and display staff on an ad hoc basis.

FITTING ROOMS

Lighting levels, color, direction, and diffusion play an enormous role on the attitude of the customer in a fitting room. Too many stores use a single overhead fluorescent which has these effects on the customer:

- *The color turns the skin green.*
- *The direction of the light creates shadows under the eyes and accentuates wrinkles.*
- *The brightness hurts the eye and is compensated by the iris diaphragm which closes down, making it harder to see the details.*

2.9

J. Byron, Florida. This niche is well presented. The slight increase in the intensity of the light helps to focus the eyes to a fixed position. The arrangement of the rest of the department is such that the directions of the merchandise arrangements augment this center position.

Dressing room lighting should glamourize the patron first, and product after. The notion of feeling good helps to sell. Good lighting provides the glamour moment of a portrait photo session. The types of lamps and fixtures used should permit:

- *Diffused light across the front of the subject at not too great an angle from the eye level. Sconce positions or multiple bulb strips around them mirror serve the purpose. This washes out most surface wrinkles.*
- *Back lighting for a halo effect. This sets the patron away from the background.*
- *Good general lighting to see the merchandise.*

Dressing rooms are small. The amount of light equates to the temperature level. No matter how glamourous the lighting, beads of perspiration are annoying and can damage the garment. The amount of heat from light sources must be balanced with air conditioning.

CASHWRAP

The last area of the store that requires a touch of theatrical ambiance is the checkout or cashwrap counter. When merchandise – especially food and Ready-to-Wear – are carried to the register, it is important to minimally maintain the color of the item that the customer saw on the sales floor.

When customers see color changes at this critical moment, they may interrupt the purchase process to check the color for accuracy of intended match or freshness. When either happens, there is a possibility that the item may be returned to stock. Here the level of brightness is less a factor than the color.

All light levels should permit some highlighting with spots or special effect lighting. The ultimate effect of a "comfortable level" of drama in planning lighting for a store or center, should create a variety of sensations from *urgency and desire to buy, to elation and entertainment.*

Chapter Three

Physiological Absolutes

People who work in stores, in all capacities, make separations between themselves and shoppers. Since we are all shoppers at one time or another, we must consider our own response to be the same as everyone else's response. The concept that "we" are the merchants, marketers, and designers, while the customers are "them," is detrimental to the understanding and the use of the following information.

Shoppers are amazingly similar to each other. Their physical systems react in highly predictable ways to a variety of stimuli. These responses cause their bodies to move in certain recognizable paths, and when making decisions, their minds to move along recognizable patterns.

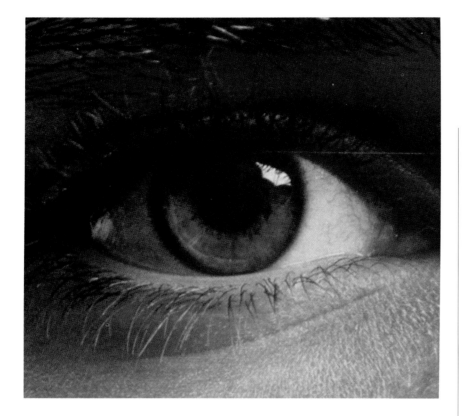

the layering of sensory input increases our ability to recall images.

Each of the senses is constantly being studied for its uniqueness and for its consistency. Our senses work on both a conscious and subconscious level. They work to define what they are sensing on a rational level. They also respond automatically and intuitively to the subtleties of the primary stimuli, as well as to related simultaneous secondary stimuli. A simple example is when the sense of smell stimulates the sense of taste.

SEEING

Seeing is the sense that transmits most images to the brain. Especially important is the visual image that forms the first impression of the shopping environment. Our eyes absorb and interpret a wide range of sensory nuances. Depth perception, color tone, clarity, height, texture, heat, and light intensity are measurable issues that are defined, wholly or partially, by our eyes. Our ability to be involved with the scene starts with an impression made by the registering of one or more visual stimuli. In addition, simultaneous recall of previously digested information that is part of our storehouse of remembrances adds our heritage to the current image.

Stimuli that influence customers' senses can be controlled to a great degree, therefore their responses are also controllable. Merchants, retail designers, and marketers who want to entice a shopper to purchase currently use only a fraction of the many sensory means to control the responses of their clientele.

SENSORY PERCEPTION

The five senses—seeing, hearing, smelling, touching, and tasting—are our physical receptors. Of the five, the sense of seeing accounts for about 90 percent of all images sent to the brain. The retention and strengthening of visual images is assisted by the overlap of other stimuli that awaken the other senses. In every instance,

The eyes can be trained to receive and interpret visual information that is pertinent to the retailer. The talent to verbalize the visual experience and communicate that knowledge to all colleagues, is the key to the ability to quickly recognize and respond to the why of customer behavior. The elements that specifically make the visual aesthetic definable in a store are:

- *Focus*
- *Vertical Image*
- *Interrupted Pattern*
- *Color*
- *Brightness (light intensity)*
- *Diagonals*
- *Volume (cubic space)*
- *Texture*
- *Rhythm*

FOCUS

Because we have two eyes that are horizontally set in our head, we actually get a registry of both images in our brain. This fact helps us to *triangulate* the focus to determine exact position. The idea of focus then is not just a two-dimensional reality, but one of three dimensions. Focus is not just lateral and vertical, but also linear in depth. The normal results of using two eyes at one time causes several specific visual priorities. We focus on singular objects. Our eyes pinpoint focus. Our eyes give us a more defined, sharper point focus than an instrument, even a camera. We may skim a surface to survey an entire picture to form opinions. However, we do see only one object in that picture at a time. The compilation of impressions from all those individual images gives us the basis for judging the visual quality of an entire scene.

Check this yourselves. Pick two objects close to you about 12" apart, or look at the diamonds on either side of this page. As you follow the directions in the caption 3.1, you can see and understand your sharp focus mechanism. Do the same with two objects far away, about three feet apart–the same phenomenon. One will be in focus and the other out-of-focus.

Translate this into what happens when a customer enters a store. They scan the scene to get an overall impression; the word ambiance has been used to describe this general feeling. However, as the eyes move across several visual planes, they stop at specific points, generally at a designated item presentation. Individual merchandise fixtures can be picked out when they are given a special treatment. The single fixture is then the key to the level of acceptance of the department. *Each fixture must have its proportionate integrity.* Treated intelligently, a single fixture can augment the shopper's positive buying attitude.

3.1

Hold the page at arm's length. Focus on one diamond–the other is out-of-focus. The same result will happen at virtually any distance.

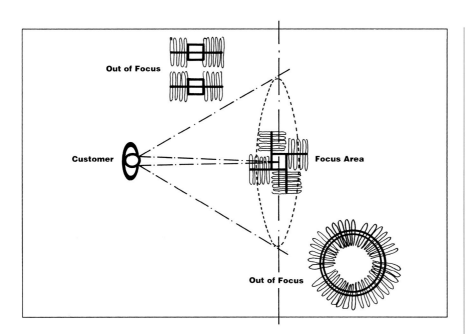

Out of Focus

Customer

Focus Area

Out of Focus

3.2

This schematic shows that the eyes focus on a point. The plane across the field of vision becomes more fuzzy at the edges. Our focusing mechanism does not focus on that plane, but adjusts for every single point along the plane.

Negative impressions of an individual presentation can be formed just as easily. Negative impressions will probably be more lasting and spread further to influence the shopper's perception of the total picture. In several instances of merchandise that is carelessly out of place, customers get a false impression of the quality of the entire department. One extreme example is the situation of a brassiere on the floor of an intimate apparel department. Even if the entire department is well presented, the eye will focus on the one piece of merchandise that is out of keeping with the whole. The impression that the customer comes away with is that it is possible that other pieces were also

on the floor, and that the stock is unsanitary. Whether a careless customer had dropped the merchandise, or if it fell because it was brushed against, the image is still the same–*negative.*

Now let's move to a more normal indication of discrepancies that can happen between the creation of the image and intent of the presentation. Even in a well-conceived store, the message received by the shopper is sometimes different from the desired image of the store. Assume that at the beginning of the day the merchandising on each fixture is reorganized and well maintained. As the day moves on, the items on that fixture start to sell down. Because of general sales activity, when there is insufficient staff, or the item is not in reserve stock, the merchandise is not, or cannot, be replaced.

What is the perception of the customer at that time? The message to the brain is distinctly not the one that the merchant wishes to present. The fixture has lost its visual integrity. Customers have stored up a history of these visual impressions that are interpreted on an ad hoc basis. *We focus on one image at a time. We absorb one image at a time. Customers use that single image as the basis for forming a general opinion.*

VERTICAL IMAGE

Often retailers tell their staff that they should merchandise in a vertical manner...color lines of towels, knit shirts, coordinated tops and bottoms, shelf merchandise, stacks of boxes, and where possible, all other items that may have a better vertical relationship. The idea of vertical presentation is quite correct, but this is only the *how* of the technique. It is far more important to explain the *why* of the action from the viewer's perspective so that the principle may be applied to other situations as well.

Let's first verify that the vertical image is dominant physiologically. Using the same basis of the reasoning that helps us to pinpoint focus, look at the diagram of concentric circles.

(3.3)

Fix your focus at the center of the circles. Now do the following without moving your focus from that point. Alternately blink the left and right eye. The horizontal image jumps more than the vertical image. Horizontally your focus moves off the page, while vertically it is held within the center of the concentric circle field. This is because both of our eyes are sending an independent message to our brain. The overlap of those images occurs in the center vertical elongated oval. The vertical image then is virtually twice as strong as the horizontal. The horizontal spread is peripheral vision. We pick up indications of pictures at the far edges of our field, but to get them into focus we either must move our eyes or turn our heads.

(3.4)

The jamming of units on one arm, or careless customers, may create an anti-aesthetic, anti-hygienic, anti-sales situation.

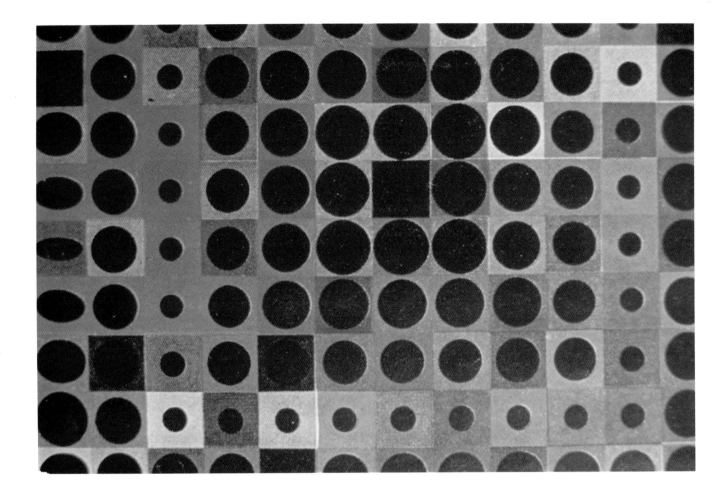

(3.5)

(Vasarely. Detail) As your eyes move across the surface, they will stop at a particular square or circle. The point generally picked is the square in the center of the group of circles. This is the result of the law of interrupted pattern. Black circles start from around the outer perimeter and graduate in diameter to the center. They form the biggest block of repeat shapes on the surface. Our eyes pick up a pattern of circles, ascending to the center. Then our senses are jarred by the unexpected–a square in the center. The artist deliberately put it there to control the viewers eye movement over the surface. The black square is the interruption in the pattern. If this weren't enough to force the eye to that spot, the square in this detail is placed in the upper right quadrant of the picture.

INTERRUPTED PATTERN

As we start to put together the elements of seeing, we can begin to understand how several of the peculiarities of sight can be applied to product presentation. The following physical phenomena has consistent, predictable reactions. It is a deliberate use of a law of aesthetics that forces the eye to move to a specific point.

The law of *interrupted pattern* simply states that the eye is drawn to an interruption in a pattern, before the brain can absorb the entire pattern. To prove this we again start by taking an eye test. Look at the section of the Vasarely painting. It is full of circles, squares, and a variety of colors. Hold the diagram as far from your eyes as possible and follow the directions in caption 3.5.

Newspapers place the lead item of the day at the upper right corner of the first page. They know that our eye movement follows our brain function. The left half of the brain is where the facts are stored. The right side of the brain is the area where we form the logic for decision making.

We literally have the ability to make people see what we want them to see. When we accomplish that, we can also create a path to make them move where we want them to move, and subsequently induce purchases

of items that we wish to sell. It is not just a mind game that we have at our control. There are ways that the use of single physical response principles, or the use of combined principles, may be used to sell merchandise at all price points, including sales.

In the presentation of men's dress shirts shown in 3.6, the bow tie attracts attention first because the eye focuses on the interruption in the pattern. The merchant has combined two of the physiological factors that we have been describing: vertical image

If you can get the customer to see what you want them to see, they will probably buy what you want to sell.

and interrupted pattern. Under the bow tie is the largest number of shirts in the assortment. Centering the bow tie has a residual automatic result of drawing the focus of both eyes to the vertical line of merchandise directly below. The items we see first are the items that we will be likely to buy first. As the group sells down, if they could not be replaced, the same technique can be applied to another line of shirts. It is not necessary to remerchandise the entire presentation. Simply move the bow tie to the next largest group of shirts in the assortment. This technique may also be used to augment the sale of a desired color.

(3.7)

Left: Melart Jewelers, Washington, DC. The neutral backing keys a more subdued, classical response for fine jewelry, seen mainly against skin.

Right: Melart Jewelers, Washington, DC. Color pads are used for colored stones, promotions, or seasonal effect.

COLOR

Color is the easiest issue for the staff to coordinate. It is also the easiest for the customers to use as an idea for style organization.

Color perception has many shades of meaning. From the mystical to the silly, color has become the *bête noire* of merchants who have no personal color references or preferences. There is no specific formula, but there is a logic to color choice that will produce given effects. Colors can be made to be pleasant or unpleasant. They can soothe or jar the senses. But the important thing to remember is what Josef Albers, a world renowned artist known for his color theories, always claimed, "Every color goes with every other color, depending on the proportion."

Colors, as with most of the elements of sensory perception, are always to be seen in a balance with other elements.

Designers are always asked, "What is the best color to go with this particular merchandise?" In making the most difficult selections in design it is *always* best to start by answering one question with another, "How does the color relate to the way the customer visualizes that product?"

Jewelry case backing and pads are always a prime category for color concern. If we consider what is the natural backing for *each* price range and classification for the category, we can come up with formulas that satisfy 80 percent of public perception.

Fine jewelry. From metals to stones and pearls, fine jewelry is generally worn in direct contact with the skin. Choose light tone, warm flesh neutrals that relate to flesh color to portray a classical elegance.

Bridge jewelry. The design of many of these pieces is potentially the element of more value than the material. Bridge jewelry can be worn against fiber or against the skin, therefore the choice for backing colors is discretionary.

Costume jewelry. This category is generally bought as a fashion accessory and becomes interdependent with the clothing and should be shown against fashion colors, preferably current-seasonal.

As you go through the assortment and the categories within the assortment it becomes apparent that most of the collection will relate more to neutral colors. High intensity, highly saturated full primary or secondary colors relate to faster-moving seasonal fashion colors. The entire shop then may be done in tones of neutrals, allowing for internal changes. Exceptions exist for colors that back certain merchandise categories, such as sporting goods, electronics, toys, and outdoor furniture. Exceptions will also exist where seasonal or promotional considerations play a more primary role, at the moment, than the longevity of the style of the item.

It is not only opaque color, or even the transparent light spectrum, that forms the final judgement of appropriate color to the merchandise. *Color perception is determined at the moment that the viewer absorbs the picture.*

Perceived ambient color is a combination of all the factors from lamp color and heat, to cubic floor density. Lamp intensity creates the number of footcandles present on the floor. That intensity and color is also affected by the reflection from the walls, floor, ceiling, merchandise, fixtures, and the *customers themselves*. The equation includes all these judgmental and learned responses combined with the technical and natural additions.

The occasional exception, one that successfully breaks the rule, can be an indication of new trends, fads, or new laws of color use. Daring merchants who linked product to the color ambiance won new audiences for their marketing, as well as fortified their own fashion position.

When the song, "Feeling Groovy" was popular, Alexander's at Lexington Avenue and 58th Street, New York City, launched a Feeling Groovy boutique on the fashion floor. The shop put together assortments for disco goers. The display team decided to cover the fluorescent tubes in the department with blue transparent plastic. The merchants accepted the idea that the less bright blue color light that related to their perception of disco lighting was, at that time, more important than the previously acceptable color and intensity. It was a successful innovation sparked by the creativity of the visual merchandise director. The lighting made the items more desirable to the customers by placing them in the ambiance of the space in which they would eventually be worn.

Color in housewares or hardware departments is generally a brighter hue. Much of this is needed to work with the color of the products or the packaging. These departments also use natural materials for departmental ambiance. Room settings and furniture areas in stores tend to be more adventurous in the proportion of brighter colors to neutrals than do actual home settings.

The color ranges of the items in a domestic department are quite wide compared to the choice of the three best selling colors. In many geographic markets, two of the three, or all three colors that sell best are white, beige, and blue. However, in order to give the appearance of selection, the store must carry, and equally display, the full color range available. The effect gives credibility to the store's belief in its own product, as well as permitting the customers their taste preference.

The favorite color of most people is red. In selecting colors, infants will reach for the red color first. Red remains the prime choice until adulthood and post-menopausal age. Color preference then generally shifts to blue. Although most people will choose these two colors when asked, very few find that they can live with these colors on a continuous basis. Therefore, most of the rooms in their homes are in neutral, light tones. It is hard for the nervous system to constantly absorb bright intensity. In fact, people tend to move faster, and stay less, in high-hued, brightly-lit rooms and departments.

Color preferences are constantly being made either verbally or unconsciously. The preferences by age, sex, background, and geography have predetermined patterns. *By tapping into the mind of the customer through the eminently powerful tool of color, we can orchestrate much of their response.*

There are laws for color use. Guidelines for general practices exist, and will work for most situations. But the visionary who breaks the rules, in a newly acceptable color aesthetic, will be the one who creates memorable stores.

BRIGHTNESS AND LIGHT INTENSITY

Eye movement in response to light intensity is an automatic physical reaction. *Our eyes move to brighter intensity.* Higher light intensity causes the eye lids to blink or shut, and the iris diaphragm to close down. This shutting down of the iris that adjusts for accidental brightness will generally lessen our ability to see the desired merchandise. However, when the right spotlighting is focused on desired merchandise, it draws our eyes to that stock.

Light intensity also affects our perception of price and value. When we are in a high-bright-intensity retail environment that primarily uses fluorescent tubing, what is the perception of price to value? Low price, but probably good value. Now place yourself into a subdued environment, moderately intense light, primarily from quartz, halogen, or tungsten. What is your perceived ratio of price to exclusivity? High price and exclusive. Add to that the quantity of stock available for selection and we start to understand how color, light (and inventory levels) effect the first perception of price, value, exclusivity, and product credibility.

When discussing intensity of light, we must consider all sources. Sunlight is the most powerful single source of light. It is also the most changeable and uncontrollable. Window lighting is a problem for most stores no matter what the window backing. On the street, or in a mall, the filtering of daylight into the store also creates a reflection in the windows that is always stronger than the image of the display or merchandise in the shop. From sunset into the night, the problem does not exist.

When controlled and used with style, sunlight is a positive force when relating to color perception.

3.8

The architecture of the shopping center is shown more clearly than the merchandise. Daylight in the courtyard will always create high reflection which will negatively affect the presentation.

(3.9)

Cemaco, Guatemala. This toy presentation features the item that is deepest in stock and expected to sell the most. The triangular presentation draws the eye to the item without looking as if the plush animal is in huge surplus.

DIAGONALS

Since we see vertical and horizontal lines throughout most of our day, we find diagonal lines particularly compelling. Many of our early memories of shopping include escalator rides. Moving diagonally through space was always the transportation mode of a retail store and enclosed mall.

Diagonals translate into the sense of movement. Diagonals lead the eye, and two juxtaposed diagonals form a pyramid. This shape guarantees that the eyes will move to the apex. Whether the pyramid is two dimensional as it would be on a wall presentation, or if it is three dimensional, as packages in stacks, those products near the top and forming the outer lines of the shape will get the most attention.

Diagonals generally refer to lines that are between 10 and 80 degrees to the vertical and horizontal. In fact, the creation of diagonal traffic aisle patterns, discussed in Chapter 5, creates this movement which merchants consider critical to department penetration.

VOLUME

Interior space scale gives us a sense of physical comfort as well as personal perspective. The entry, or foyer, of a store or department, is where the customer first judges the amount of cubic space to merchandise density. For example, the distance from the viewer to the object can be set so that the viewer gives an added value to the subject. Our eyes do not focus on items that are placed too close to an entry. In art, as in retail, the merchant must set the presentation so that there is an *aesthetic distance* between the viewer and the object to be viewed.

Through the perception of volume and space, we get a most unusual sense of merchandise propriety. What we see and what we think about inventory, price, exclusivity, and freshness comes from our mental image of the spatial balance. Some stores with the least number of items per cubic area are the highest in sales per square foot, because they com-

bine ambient elegance and exclusivity with sales service. Other stores with low inventory levels that do not have elegance and sales service just look to be out-of-stock.

Aisles in a department that is mid-priced must be wide enough to pass but not too wide to give the perception of higher-priced products than that the store is known for.

Supermarkets are about the best example of merchandise presented in a cavernous space. The produce they sell must turn 24 times a year or it rots. To keep the visual balance of space to product, they drop the ceiling and raise the items off the floor—and they build dummy pyramids on the tables to give more vertical/diagonal visual presence to the items. This permits a fullness to the presentation, and keeps the on-hand inventory relatively low. Good supermarkets always look full, with fresh products in full rotation on the shelves and tables.

TEXTURE

Although texture is always considered to be determined by the sense of touch, it can be first detected by the eyes. Lighting is the major factor in creating visual surface changes. Just the verbal description of each surface can evoke a mental picture of a textural difference, and in each we also see the lighting that creates that difference. Think of the following surface textures, and conjure up the image:

(3.10)

Byerly's, Minneapolis. Lighting also controls the direction of sight. We are propelled to look first at the merchandise. The glamour of the entire area adds to the desirability of the product. In fact, this supermarket chain also sells crystal and porcelain gifts. There is a believable linkage between the elegance of the presentation of food to the exclusive gifts.

(3.11)

Coin, Italy. A shallow department can successfully increase it percieved depth by sculpting the merchandise.

- *Silk*
- *Sheer lace*
- *Nubby wool knits*
- *Velvet*
- *Chintz*
- *Twine*
- *Gossamer*
- *Plastic*
- *Matting*

RHYTHM

As the eyes focus from point to point, it becomes apparent that the more we can make the vision flow easily to the place that we want the customers to look, the better chance we will have to hold their attention. The merchandise and the fixtures fill a volume. It is more pleasing to go from high to low, from staccato to smooth, from mass to detail.

In photo 3.11, the fixtures are set to let the face-outs of the jackets read in a step pattern from the aisle to the display on the wall. It is a one, two, three, four arrangement that makes the customer's eyes easily flow to the desired presentation. The horizontal wall presentation is arranged in varying height in an up-down rhythm that coincides at the same place as the front-to-back rhythm. The face-outs on the wall are flanked by bulk shoulder hang. The highest point is the prime focus. The remainder of the stock on the floor fills out the stock to hold basic fashion merchandise in quantity without looking like a markdown is coming. It is a strong fashion presentation with stock width and depth for an upper-middle market.

CONCLUSION

Cultural information digested through our experiences form the logic of emotional, intuitive responses. We form opinions, and try to verify those ideas, using the combination of physical and psychological data that comes through seeing. Seeing gives us the first and most important impression. You do not get a second chance to make a first impression. But, the eyes do not operate alone as message receivers and transmitters of information to the brain. All of our other senses contribute independently and collectively to image making.

We learn more each year about the sophistication and the reliability of other senses. The retention of images gets stronger and more memorable as the other senses receive impulses that form a single sensory experience.

Chapter Four

Support Sensitivities

Each of the five senses can produce a response that will encourage a shopper to buy more merchandise.

Although 90 percent of all images sent to the brain originate with seeing, other senses play an important support role. There are many instances when the senses of hearing, smell, taste, and touch are the first stimuli to register in the brain.

A single perception by one sense has characteristics that are distinct from the others. Stimulating a sensory response can initiate a process that recalls an image already stored, or can create a new image record. Each of the senses can also trigger a physical response from another sense, without the direct involvement of the other.

The effect of marketplaces on consumers becomes exciting when all the senses are concurrently aroused by engulfing sensory stimuli. That was the joy of the bazaars, souks, and agoras of history. Each market intensifies the sensory delights of the region, many of which are also found in the home. The rationale for the deliberate use of sensory stimuli in retail is based on reminding customers of recognizable, pleasant, positive feelings. *Combinations of sensory stimuli can produce harmonious balances that induce a customer to stay longer, and shop more.*

Any idea of customer comfort levels relates to surroundings that evoke pleasant memories. There are volumes written on the anatomical receptors that receive and transmit messages from each distinct sense. The following information uses the technical aspects of these works to show application for practical use on the selling floor.

SOUND

Sound is the curtain raiser, the overture, the stimulating mind pre-set that opens the path to customer acceptance.

Sound is most frequently linked with sight. Our culture, as it has developed in the twentieth century, relies on the combination of audio-visual communications to transmit its most memorable images. Movies, even silent films with a piano accompaniment, and modern television have been produced to create a super-charged atmosphere. Words, music, and special effects combine with a variety of visual sights to fight for a space in our memory bank.

Sound, like smell, possesses a quality unmatched by the other three senses. It is multi-dimensional. It can travel around corners and can be detected without any direct recognition of the source. Marketplace sounds can be heard by a customer riding on an escalator before reaching a position where the merchandise may be seen. Moods and attitudes change as retailers change the music heard in one department from another. *The sound that induces more customers to get a positive sensation is the sound of people talking.*

Customers are generally subdued when shopping. When they shop in pairs, they are rarely overheard. However, when customers cluster around a fixture that has highly desirable new stock or an irresistible price point, they talk louder and more excitedly. The sound of their voices brings other customers to the area.

Salespeople who know their product are more likely to talk about it. When other customers overhear this conversation, they raise their credibility level about the product, the salesperson, and the store.

Many businesses use sound or sound control to achieve certain responses. Its message is almost totally subliminal. Yet, responses created by similar sounds have predictable patterns. Although there may be different interpretations of music by different people, there are definite acceptable parameters that lie within the range of customer acceptance.

Certain rhythms and melody types will encourage customers to shop more slowly and move more casually, increasing the feeling of comfort.

Muzak has been around for 55 years and has made quantifiable studies. Researchers have recorded the physical and psychological results. They search for classical and popular music that has been calculated to create an air of well-being. Musak is now programmed in a "stimulus progression" in order to elevate the spirits. Other studies by Musak show that customers spend more time shopping and, subsequently, spend more money when they hear pleasing, recognizable music.

Music can change ambient sound to relate to particular styles of merchandise. Even a small specialty store can use different music within the same space. For the employees, it is important to vary the sound to prevent it from becoming numbing. There is morning, afternoon, and

4.1

Nouvelle Galeries, France. This customer is smelling the fiber of the shirt to determine quality. He remembers when shirts were made of natural fibers that had sweet and distinctive smells. Unfortunately, this shirt is a man-made fiber and has no smell.

evening music. Most radio stations program their sound accordingly.

There should be a layering of many sounds in a store: music, customers talking, salespeople explaining product, escalators, and of course the highlight of a retailer's day—the sound of the cash register.

AROMA

Aromas, like sound, can travel around corners and can be detected without physical contact of the source. Smell is primitive. Reaction to smell is instantaneous. Aromas arouse hormonal production which cause physical response. These aromas, which often relate to the home, are prime factors in making customers feel comfortable in a commercial space.

The management of Mrs. Fields Cookies Shoppes has computerized data, constantly selecting by store location statistics showing the

(4.2)

**Mrs. Fields. The
"down-home"
appearance masks
the highly skilled use
of electronic
information to make
smell a continuous
factor in customers'
decision-making.**

number of customers likely to enter on any day. The dual purpose of this is to keep the ovens in use to maintain an aroma level, and to keep the cookies fresh.

Real estate agents recommend putting bread or an apple pie in the oven before showing a home to a prospective buyer. They say that the pleasant aromas will "cover the cracks on the wall."

In northern temperate zones, we are stimulated to buy by the smell of apples and cinnamon. In southern tropical climates coffee smells do the same. In a North American supermarket chain, the managers are instructed to grind a pound of coffee every morning and sprinkle it on the floor in the sawdust near the cash register. Any aromas that recall a pleasant home environment create a comfort level that allows us to feel at ease.

Perfumes and home fragrances are sometimes (but not often enough) used in entrances. There are stores that deliberately use aroma to sensually and legally seduce their clientele. Aromas have an associative relevance that can be surprisingly similar to groups of people. What comes to mind when the following aromas are mentioned?

- *Cinnamon–homecooking, warm, family, cozy*
- *Coffee–home cooking, warm, family, cozy*
- *Apples–home cooking, warm, family, cozy*
- *Fragrance–sensuous, evening*
- *Orange–healthy, bright*
- *Garlic–yummy, ethnic*
- *Mildew–damp, basement*
- *Pine–country, outdoors, healthy*
- *Leather–quality, West, new car*
- *Gasoline– auto parts*
- *Earth–pastoral, outdoors*
- *Flowers–honeysuckle, roses, hyacinth, paper white, lily-of-the-valley, gardenias–fresh, romantic*
- *Baby- freshly bathed, talc*
- *Fresh paint–turpentine, clean*
- *Wood–general country hardware store*
- *Sawdust–beer, barroom, crafted items*
- *Fabric–cotton, linen, wool–sweet*
- *Lemon–fresh, clean*
- *Fire–wood burning, camping, warmth*
- *Ocean–salt air, refreshing*

The technical aspect of smell is fascinating. We are not conscious of the actions taken by our bodies in recognizing and codifying smell. Our sense of smell is determined by two levels of recognition. The first level identifies whether the smell is pleasant or not. The second level then identifies the specific smell, to mentally locate the most memorable time we experienced that smell, and place it geographically as well.

We can differentiate between 10,000 different aromas. We can recall a smell after 50 years. We can be aroused sexually by smell. We can be made to feel comfortable by smell. We can become hungry by smell. We can be nauseated by smell. We can be induced to buy by smell. We augment, and indeed permit, our taste buds to function by smell. We can be directed toward smell without any other sense functioning. All retail activities may be enhanced by the use of related smells. *Properly used, smell stimulates sales.*

(4.3)

Victoria's Secret always combines many sensual stimuli to provoke a sexual imagery in a pseudo-Victorian ambiance. The catalogs stop short of being a fantasy. The merchandise, the ambiance, and the personnel work well together for this division of The Limited.

TOUCH

Where is the first place in the store that we experience touch? What body mechanism is the receptor for this stimuli?

When walking into a store toward a product presentation, we get numerous touch signals from the way that the floor surface changes. From concrete, to marble, to wood, to tile, to carpet, *the surface under our feet gives us the first indication of change of location. Even blindfolded, we can tell change in surface density and texture. Walking from a main aisle to a carpeted presentation, a customer's attitude can be directed toward the merchandise.*

There are several instances of surface texture uses where the designer has deliberately changed or maintained surface texture in order to get a predetermined disposition from the customer. In Treviso, Italy, the home of Benetton, one of their shops on the street used the same street pavement material across the threshold of the store. A mall shop can continue center court tile into the main traffic aisle. These designs create an easy transition for the client.

Quite the opposite was done in another store. The designer of the swim shop shown on the next page considered the floor surface of the swim shop before placing the fixtures. On top of existing carpet, wood planking was used to relate to a boardwalk at the beach. (Two more obvious textures, water and sand, could have been used but would be considerably less practical.) Overhead light was added later and filtered through blue gauzy fabric creating a mottled quality of underwater light. The designer added appropriate sunny summer afternoon music and pine and salt air scent that combine to make us think of outdoors, ocean, and feeling healthy.

A lingerie shop can use incandescent light, area carpets over wood, peach-colored fabric with wall paint to match, and a variety of aromas from pot pourri to sachets on hangers, to perfume, to set the atmosphere seductively to present "sexy" intimate apparel.

TASTE

Except where food is the product, and the definition of "taste" is literal, we could try to define "taste" in terms of acceptable "good taste" and unacceptable "bad taste." These terms are used frequently with the tacit understanding that there is agreement to their meaning.

Have you ever tried to define "taste"? Whether describing a single item or an ambiance created by the juxtaposition and/or the overlay of many stimuli, what makes the acceptance "good taste" or the disturbance "bad taste?" So far the best definition has to do with balances, rhythms, and sequence. In a basic sense, good taste is an acceptance of previously determined commonalities. Good taste can

Rheinbrucker, Switzerland. In this department, the customer is given a wonderful sense of aesthetics in the rhythm and the movement of all the elements. The arms on the fixtures slope in a diagonal that counterbalance the action of the swimming and diving mannequins. The repetition of items shown on the arms of the fixtures creates an effect similar to that of a strobe light, furthering the sense of movement.

also refer to judgements made of a situation or an object not previously encountered. If an observation is made where an element, or several elements, are out of place to the personal acceptable norm, but not jarring to expectations, then the general feeling is that the whole is acceptable. Even new unexpected experiences can be pleasant, and therefore another degree of acceptable good taste.

When a sequence of perceptions becomes jarring, irrational, and difficult to comprehend, it becomes bad taste. All of this is a psychological evaluation and explanation of physical phenomena that can induce physical response.

Classically coordinated aesthetics will always find a level of acceptance. In use without variation, they can also produce negative feelings of boredom. The degree of acceptable variety that a designer adds to the offering will make the space package more enticing to the customer. *Memorable good taste will always be a blend of the intuitively acceptable with pleasant surprises.* It can also be guaranteed that the specific parameters of all taste will change from time to time, place to place, culture to culture, and age to age.

CONCLUSION

The five senses can be trained to increase greater degrees of sensitivities. Understanding them and their use by the merchant and the designer will provide many of the answers to why customers behave in a certain manner. It will put into words the feelings of non-verbal customers. It helps the buying staff understand the need to evaluate the price–value equation. The language of retail must be consistent and easily understandable.

The best way to use a language of retail aesthetics is to employ emotions that start from the human experience. *Making a verbal analogy between store staff and store clientele that expresses these experiences, is the most direct and memorable method for the highest retention of all information.*

Chapter Five

Traffic Patterns

esign for retail begins with the entry to the store and the movement of the customer through the selling space. Walking equates positively to sales. Sales levels are in a direct proportion to the distance covered in the store, not the time spent. *Designers can create traffic flow patterns that will absolutely increase the possibility of deeper department and store penetration.*

Shoppers who move while they shop are called browsers. Shoppers who spend time in a store without moving are called frustrated. Designers must be aware of the predictable actions of the great majority of people who come to buy. It is the designer's job to facilitate entry, continuous movement, the creation of merchandise pictures, the selection of merchandise, purchase, and exit.

**Gap Kids. The plan
of this store forces
most customers to
start moving to
the right.**

THE CUSTOMER
ALWAYS TURNS RIGHT

In order to complete a favorable impression of the entire transaction, the designer must first assume the role of a merchant while seeing the space as a customer. The predictable actions of most shoppers provide designers with the initial keys to space planning. In this chapter we will discuss physical tendencies and limitations that dictate the parameters of designing selling space.

In the previous two chapters, we have seen why customers have developed an attitude toward the store. Once they enter the store, customers are within the control zone that can be manipulated by the merchant or the store designer. *When entering any space, most people, without a specific destination in mind, will turn to the right. In fact, 80 percent or more will turn to the right.* This is dictated by the function of the brain and has little to do with right and left handedness.

We absorb and digest information in the left part of the brain. We assimilate and logically use this information in the right half of the brain. When we scan a scene, we look from left to right and generally fix on an object, on the right, essentially at a 45 degree angle from the point that we enter. Once focused on this object we move toward it if the path is clear. The depth and overall sense of space determines how far we must penetrate from the portal before we even start to scan.

Therefore, a human factor of "proportional acceptance" is used by the shopper prior to reaching the first scanning point. The variation of the "foyer" or welcoming space is noted in the accompanying diagram.

In order to comprehend the repetitiveness of customer actions, I recommend that designers *go shopping.* They should walk into stores of all sizes and price points. *They should observe the customers entering and moving, and convince themselves that the customer is always right, figuratively and literally.*

Large Store 100,000 Sq. Ft.

Specialty Store 2,000 Sq. Ft.

The prior section on seeing demonstrated that the eye focus mechanism sharply pinpoints objects at any depth. This fact must be utilized by merchants who must be permitted by the design to make presentation statements with merchandise, not architecture.

Aisle configuration must allow access to each department and logical adjacency flow from point to point with enticing merchandise presentations no more than 20 to 30 feet apart. The orchestration of customer movement coordinates with enticing visual merchandise presentation. As customers see and move, they do not move in a line, but rather meander and will "bounce" from sequential points that are within the control sphere of designers and merchants.

However deep the store or each department, most customers will hesitate before entering an area that does not have a visual termination at 25 to 30 feet. Psychologically fearful of being "trapped," they must also sense an exit pattern before entering.

Shop Size Sq. Ft.	Foyer Size	Foyer Sq. Ft.	Percent of Total Area
2,000	8 x 10	80	4.0
3,000	9 x 12	108	3.5
10,000	10 x 15	150	1.5
100,000	12 x 20	240	0.0024

(5.2)

Foyer plans and proportion chart. The percentage of space needed by a customer to operate in varies in a downward geometric ratio as the size of the store increases.

(5.3)

A, B: Bounce plans. The eye movement, or bounce plan, can show where to position the best selling departments.

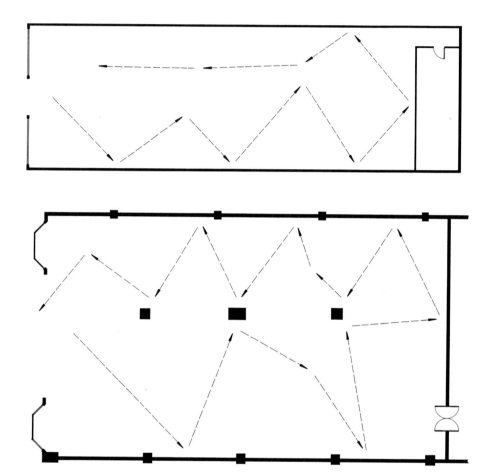

A: Even without columns, aisles can be created to make islands.

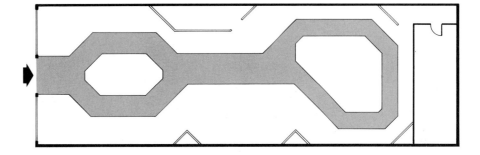

B: Plan, columns and aisles, specialty store. Notice how the aisles are placed using the columns as center points of island departments. This technique benefits smaller spaces because it can impact limited, more focussed merchandise.

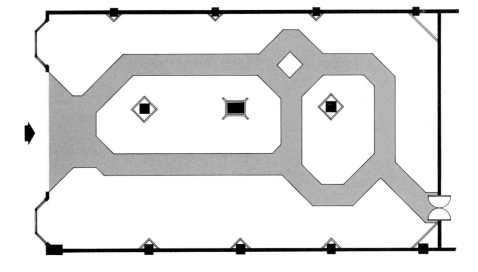

C: Plan, columns and aisles, large store. The same basic column and aisle principle holds for larger spaces.

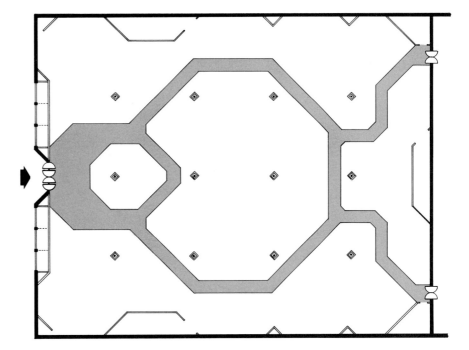

M Store, Montreal. Even in a store with many columns, the management felt that another column would be useful. They made one with four grid screens. The simple display at the top is used as the sign.

FIXED FEATURES OF LARGE STORES

What are fixed architectural features? The entrance position, the walls, and the columns. These three issues are considered with the main traffic aisle plan. Most stores use an aisle directly in from the main entry. Large stores with distinct and different merchandise categories use large wide aisles to separate major category changes.

However, some mall anchor stores continue these large aisles from entry to exit in a straight path. In shopping centers, these aisles go from parking lot to center court, making the store a speedway convenience for the specialty shops. The inability to divert the path and attention of people walking through the store and turn them into shoppers is a loss for merchants.

UTILIZING COLUMNS

The underutilization of columns in mid-floor is possibly the greatest loss of potential sales. What troubles a plan most is the historically unfounded idea that center floor columns are obstructions that should, at best, be clad with mirror and be used as markers for aisle patterns. In most current construction, columns are about 40 to 50 feet on center, the general distance from the wall to one of the main traffic aisles of large stores. Many store planners almost automatically place the column on either side of an aisle, and the department winds up to be either 40 or 50 feet deep. The depth can be reduced by the placement of stockrooms, dressing rooms, offices, or utility areas. In one shop, a designer convinced the owner to spend an additional $250,000 to engineer a system that did away with perfectly useful center floor columns.

Columns are rare in mall specialty shops because the architects and designers of mall shops have put the operating sales areas between the support columns of the structure. Even center passages of malls are designed to fit from column to column with the facades of the stores falling out on a column line. This has worked well for the mall developers whose center aisle common spaces and shops are rarely wider than 40 feet. However, the use of a device such as a column that can attract center floor attention is also of value to specialty shops.

Columns can have a higher calling than to hold up the ceiling. Some stores have even added wing walls onto columns to increase their highly potent merchandise capability. Not all columns need to be used. Some columns may be buried in center floor dressing or stock rooms. But columns can be set with merchandise to be the strong selling idea of the category and the story of the current style in that category.

What types of columns are best to hold merchandise? Depending on the department, structure or cladding, a column should accommodate enough presence of merchandise to identify a potential new best seller or standard selling high velocity basic. Most support columns, square or round, measure 6-8 inches in diameter. The width of a column with cladding designed to hold merchandise should be approximately 36 inches so it can hold two garments faced out, or a reasonable width of vertically stacked shelf merchandise.

The orientation of the axis of the columns should be 45 degrees to the main traffic flow. Cladding around columns permits this angle around pre-existing architectural columns. Columns set at 90 degrees to the traffic flow only show one side well from the aisle. (The importance of the 45 degree angle is shown at the conclusion of this section.)

Columns are the highest point in the center floor of the store. As the eyes will focus on high points, the merchandise on a column will be the first merchandise seen, increasing the chances of its being bought. The rate of sale of merchandise presented on a column is from two to eight times normal levels, whether RTW, shampoo, fry pans, or sewing thread.

UTILIZING WALLS

Equal to the column in merchandise importance is the wall. The height and extent of the wall make it the most formidable fixture for the full variety of purposes in a store. *The concept of departmental penetration is to get customers to move to the wall.* The advantages of these actions are:

- *Once at the wall, customers have passed many items shown on floor stands.*
- *Customers are then out of the main traffic pattern and will shop more slowly.*
- *Customers will see more items for choice and will buy more items at full margin.*
- *When finished selecting merchandise, customers will turn to the main aisle and exit the department. On the way they see the other 50 percent of the stock housed on the back of floor fixtures.*

Walls hold more merchandise than any other fixture in the department. Properly used, it is the merchandise sign of the department, showing the category and the current style issue, and should be the first concern of the presentation. *It is the most valuable tool in the arsenal of all in-store merchandise presentation.*

(5.6)

Debenhams, U.K. The combination of the width of the column wraps and the aisles made the columns center floor focal points.

Nouvelle Galeries, France. In this wonderfully composed presentation, the aisle between the fixture and the column leads the customer to the merchandise on the wall. Note how the manager used the white tie on a dark shirt to create an interruption in the top row pattern.

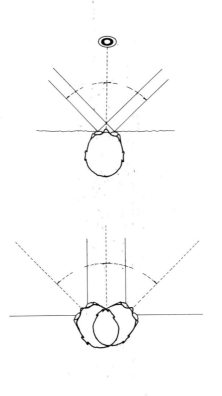

(5.7)

A. Eye movement.

B. Head movement.

AISLE PLANNING

Why is 45 degrees so important in planning aisles? The accompanying diagram tests your response. Stand at the entrance to a room. Without turning your head move your eyes from left to right. Note the farthest clear point on either side, approximately 45 degrees from the straight line. Now keep your eyes focused at a point directly in front. While keeping your eyes focused at a center point, straight ahead, move your head left then right until there is resistance. The same points are clear, 45 degrees is all you comfortably see.

Turning your head and looking extreme right or left simultaneously will permit you to see a point 90 degrees from the direct front. When you walk, it is easier to execute a 45 degree turn that a 90 degree turn.

The eye leads the body. You must see something before choosing to move towards it.

SHIFTING BUYING ATTITUDES

The customer's buying attitude changes from the entry to the exit of a store or a department. Timing, distance, and enticement affects the placement of merchandise in the store and in each department. When customers enter, they are ready to learn about a product, or to try it. Once they have reached a halfway point, they have "exit" on their mind, and their mental shopping time grows shorter. *Merchandise placement on entry and exit patterns must take into account this shift in buying attitude.*

Customers establish a fixed period of time to be used for shopping. They enter either to find a basic item or to make a fortuitous fashion find. *Whether the shopper's objective is a deliberate purchase, browsing, or to be entertained, the traffic pattern created by the designers should lead the customer to, through, and past as much-intelligently-presented merchandise as possible.*

Information Gathering

The following chapter is based on my field experience, and is therefore subjective. It involves the style of the designer, the familiarity with the staff, and the point-of-view that the designer takes. It is also meant to establish the designer as a knowledgeable merchant. The process of information gathering starts with the operating head of the firm. The merchandising mission of each company is stated by the CEO and is supported and implemented by all employees. "Quality for value" is not the mission, but the goal of all efforts. The overriding issue must be encapsulated in a short, clearly defined message that puts the owner/operator's beliefs into the eye of the public. The company then molds this image around that expressed conviction.

I stress the involvement of the president. With the direction and approval of the managing director, or CEO, from the first discussion, the information flows more easily to the completion of the project. With that understanding, a designer may concentrate on the aesthetic issues that are then carried through the technical and final phases of planning into installation. Without a mission statement and commitment from the CEO, the design will probably be turned over to a committee of peer level executives, each of whom has valid comments, but no primacy. The lateral movements of the design team will then be time consuming and counter-productive.

Spend as much time with the CEO as he or she can give, and listen. Ask questions. Have some backup questions or continuation comments in mind. Prepare your list of basic questions. Each situation will demand a variation of emphasis. Some of the suggestions are stated following each question.

- *Where are the strong points of the company?*
  Are they more interested in service, fashion, or category dominance in their market?
- *What stores are the keenest competition?*
  By location?
  By price ?
  By merchandise?

- *Where does the CEO shop and why?*
- *What stores does the CEO respect and why?*
  (This may point to future goals.)
  Are there plans for the future that should be considered?
  How does it affect the design?
- *What is the structure of the organization?*
  How many people are brought in to make decisions?

Questions asked should be devised to open up a line of mutual discussion. After all the verbal communication, the designer must still put the sentiments of the CEO into a visual form.

ESTABLISHING THE CEO'S TRUST

When the CEO and the designer start to agree on the likes and dislikes of stores, a key trust is established. The taste level and the intellect of the CEO will give the designer many clues to the details of design and the manner of presentation. It is the ultimate responsibility of the CEO to make the initial policy statement that will serve as the guiding concept throughout the project. It is essential to speak to the CEO at the beginning. Any other method leaves open the possibility of second-guessing the later decisions.

GENERAL MERCHANDISING MANAGER (GMM)

The GMM may sometimes be the owner and CEO. In that case, it is best to try to separate the functions as diplomatically as possible. Once the mission statement is established, the following questions should be answered:

- *What is the current assortment?*
  List the categories. What is the proportion of sales, actual and anticipated of each category?
- *Which merchandise categories are the core, and essential to maintain as the main customer draw?*
- *What opportunities are there for market penetration?*
- *What is the strength of the competition?*

DIVISIONAL MERCHANDISE MANAGERS (DMM) AND BUYERS

At this point, the designer should have enough information to ask and receive very specific information at divisional and buyer levels. Even though some divisionals will have multiple merchandise responsibilities, try to have distinct category separation with each divisional responsibility, and each group of buyers. *Have DMMs prepare an overview of the cat-*

egory, *including a recent history, and the targeted customers.* The questions to ask include:

- **What is the proportion of basic (year-round, durable, rarely marked-down) to fashion merchandise?**
- **What is the general cycle of style and delivery?**
  What are the best selling items in each category, by unit and by category?
- **Who are the suppliers?**
  Are their names important enough to be shown to the customers?
- **Which items, through the history of the company, may be out-of-stock most often?**
- **Is off-floor storage necessary?**
- **What form of communication, if any, is used to alert the floor staff to new arrivals?**

STORE MANAGER

During the information-gathering process, you should visit the stores. This puts a more realistic frame around the responses. It is also quite possible that there are discrepancies between what is being said and what exists in the field.

An appointment with the store manager gives an overview of the field operation. Many store managers have come up through the ranks and have first-hand experience with both the store's management and the customers. They also have a perspective on the assortment width as it applies to the actual space, and deal with the practical realities of staff training, deliveries, security, and customers.

One of the most enlightening moments of my career occurred when I asked a store manager to describe how customers shopped. The answer became the core to future studies, new theories, and finally my policy. The question was, "Tell me how your customers shop?" This store manager took me to the primary store entry from the the mall, and said that the majority of his customers entered here from the right side, and exited the same portals from the left. This simple disclosure started a progression of discussions about department positions.

To the right of the entry was the Children's Department, and on the left was the updated Sportswear Department. In terms of image, sales, and sequence, the position was wrong. The image that was intended to be given by management through the merchandise was reversed!

In a sense, the store manager is the link between the central office policy and its execution on the sales floor. Walk the store with the manager to get a sense of the staff's rapport with each other and with the management. A sharp-eyed designer will see and evaluate many of the following issues to prepare for work in a redesign or new store.

- **How good is the maintenance of the stock?**
- **What is the staff and buyer involvement?**
- **Are the areas the correct size for the merchandise content... for the customer action?**
- **Is there a need for rethinking the category potential?**
- **Are there enough cash registers? Does the customer have to wait for this important service?**
- **Are storage areas needed?**
- **Can you use more merchandise in depth...in width?**
- **How would you assess the effect on category potential?**

- **Is there a need for more staff for maintenance or service? Does this agree with the previously stated service policy?**

After making a tour with the store manager and being introduced to the staff, continue the tour alone. My general feeling about discussions is not to mix peer levels, and if possible, to allow some private feelings to emerge. Very few staff members will speak seriously about any matters in front of their bosses, or sometimes even in front of peers. Designers will probably be initially looked upon as outsiders, even if they are part of the central operating staff. The interviews and the visits should present designers as concerned and neutral professionals.

DEPARTMENT MANAGER

In the first interview with the department manager (another will follow in a second stage), you can ask some of the nitty-gritty questions needed to proceed with the technical planning.

- **Do the fixtures properly show the current assortment?**
- **Does the width of each sub-category need more or less exposure?**
- **Describe the customers' appearance and dress?**
- **How do you merchandise the area for sales...for clearances?**
- **Is there need for signing on fixtures?**
- **How many dressing rooms are needed during the busiest hours?**
- **For a hard goods or a home department, is there need for a tester area?**
- **Are the floor fixtures movable?**

I deliberately split the on-site interviews with those in the central offices, rather than interviewing one group, finishing, and then doing the other. This gives me the chance to see if the words used with one group are comprehended and acted on by the other. It also supplies a broader, more specific base for understanding the working of the organization in actual practice.

When you walk the store, you have an opportunity to see first-hand how the customers enter, shop, buy, and leave. During one data-gathering session, the CEO and I stood far enough away from the entry to watch the eye and body movement of the shoppers. We saw people walk in, move their eyes from place to place, and generally settle on one grouping in that area. The large percentage of shoppers and browsers moved to this area even when we changed the merchandise, but kept the relative importance of the presentation equal to other floor set-ups.

Make no assumptions about customers. In this chain, even with careful market planning, the customer who was the *intended* target was *less important in numbers* and buying power than the actual shoppers.

Personal tours and on-site observations should take place twice: once at the busiest times, and then at a slower time. With this variation, a designer will start to understand the need for aisle width and traffic flow. A noon-time visit may bring customers shopping with baby carriages, and require more aisle room than the evening when there are more actual shoppers. This research gives the designer a first-hand knowledge and an instant rapport with the merchants in the central offices and in the store. It also removes the stigma that the designer is dealing only in abstractions and construction materials.

VISUAL MERCHANDISING DIRECTOR (VM)

I reserve the final interview for the Visual Merchandising Director. This position has changed in the past few decades, both in title and in responsibility. VM's form the bridge that shows off the stock in a manner that is desired by the buyers, and can be maintained by the sales staff. Add the theatrical and graphic responsibility, and you are dealing with a person who is a key component of the floor presentation.

The need to differentiate between similar stores is the first step to associative merchandise identity. The art of merchandise presentation and display is essential to the clarity of the store image. *From new fashion presentation on the sales floor, to institutional and holiday purposes, the VM must be permitted to use the store as a stage to express the quality projection of the store.*

Every company that I know uses a slightly different system for the work of the visual merchandising team.

- *Where is the prep work done?*
- *Is there need for in-store storage or work space?*
- *Where would you put electrical outlets or track lighting relative to windows and the interior?*
- *Would workshops in each store facilitate the work?*
- *What do they think about competition, and where do they shop?*
- *Does the store use mannequins in the interior?*
- *Does the store sell merchandise from the display?*
- *Are there swing areas needed for new merchandise, boutiques, or special promotions?*
- *Is there a need for display storage or workroom?*
- *What is the policy on the use of demonstrators?*

RESEARCH BENEFITS

It sounds like a lot of time and work to gather the information, but there is no substitute for doing your own legwork. *An understanding of the thrust of the company's policy, from the CEO to the sales staff, will invariably save days at the drawing board.*

Chapter Seven

Planning For A Change

The major work for many store designers is renovation and redesign involving the physical changes of the department itself. It is part of, but different from, the design and construction of totally new space. The premises and the process are similar, but *the major difference is that the area already has a history of sales, regardless of the category of merchandise.*

It is an opportunity to join merchants in accepting the challenge of improving sales. In the same space on a comparative basis, with the same merchandise or a new category, designers can test their aesthetics in the field of customer response and sales results. It is an evaluation that equalizes design with more direct, more easily digested merchant-oriented standards.

TYPES OF RENOVATIONS

There are three types of renovations in which designers may participate. They do not differ in scope, but in budget. One involves the gutting of an existing area; another is a cosmetic change, leaving most, or all of the decorative and structural elements in place. The third is remerchandising using the same fixtures, and basically the same space, without physical change. Designers are rarely involved in this resetting of merchandise.

All three present similar opportunities for increasing sales, and should be understood by the designer from capital outlay for purchases and labor to potential sales results.

In the information gathering process, the concentration is naturally on the demised area. However, information about adjacent departments, sister departments in other outlets, and competition adds to designer's effectiveness. This information may show that there are newer, simpler, and more cost effective ways of making the same merchandise look more appealing to changing customer taste.

Before starting the process, do some field work to learn about the culture of the store, its staff, and the acceptance of the merchandise category by the market. I have found that most chains are consistently inconsis-

tent. When store management does not espouse a policy of logic, rather than forcing mindless dictatorial central control, the ad hoc staff decision become anarchic. If there is more than one store in the company, you should visit several in the same market area.

It is amazing how much the visual appearance of each department can tell you about the potential and the actual sales of those departments. Go equipped with sales history and projections. In the selected departments, observe trends in category and unit sales, and note the best department in:

- *Total volume*
- *Percent of annual growth*
- *Fixture use by item*
- *Stock maintenance*

Note the lowest in each category as well. If possible, obtain the following information with a year-to-date comparison.

- *Inventory by:*
  a. value
  b. SKU (Stock Keeping Unit)
  c. Number of units on hand (on sales floor and in reserve)
- *Sales by:*
  a. Number of transactions (daily and weekly)
  b. Average value per transaction
  c. Number of units per transaction

d. Sales of adjacent departments

e. Best unit sales of any item per category

f. Best unit sales by value

- *Number of turns by:*

  a. department

  b. category

- *Rank of department by contribution to store sales*

Try to obtain these figures by department compared to the total company. Develop a staff organizational diagram. With a few questions about who does the merchandising of the store, with emphasis on the presentation, you can determine how much responsibility the central offices or the store staff have to the merchandise presentation function.

SCOPE OUT THE COMPETITION

Discuss the competition with the department manager or the floor manager. Visit competitors' stores and evaluate their strengths. Customer action is a major consideration. Look closely at that activity before judging the store's design.

Sometimes the sales figures of other stores are available through in-house or industry sources. These sales statistics will often justify your observations.

TEST THE WATERS

Return to the store and walk in as if you were a customer. (Do not come into the selling space through the employee's entrance at the back to start the walk. This literally puts you in a disoriented starting point that is the reverse of the norm for customers.) See if the pattern that you have to take to reach the department is interesting and easy to follow. Note the signing or displays used as indicators. Once in the department, record where your eyes stop first. This is not so easy, because we (as do most customers) tend to respond from learned expectations rather than from objective physiological stimuli.

In performing this exercise, try any device that takes away the subject matter of a single item. Squint to blur the image. Scan the area quickly, and note the first time that your sight is arrested. Is it a mannequin group, or the light from the wall valance?

Now, reverse the procedure and observe customers approaching and entering the area. Look at their eye movements. Are they smooth, with perceptible pauses, or are they jerky and seemingly unfocused? Observe how and where they walk, and how they approach the merchandise.

Do they stop at the entry of an area, scan, proceed, and stop again?

Do they touch the merchandise without really looking at it?

Do they move off the aisle and penetrate to the wall?

Do not be overwhelmed by reputations. Go to a competitor's shop and observe customers' eye movements. Watch how customers look at merchandise and handle items without concentrating as their eyes wander aimlessly over an unfocused presentation. Most customers will be in and out of the store without purchasing.

CUSTOMERS' BODY LANGUAGE

Try to recognize a sequence of eye and body movement. Observe what most customers look at and move toward first, and then proceed on to other areas. Can you discern a reasonably similar sequence? Examine the merchandise and the presentation in these areas. See how many shoppers walk past and do not enter, even if they seem to look in.

What stock do customers who enter touch, pick up, and purchase, as opposed to those customers who walk in and leave without any contact with the stock? What happens after a shopper buys an item? Do they continue to shop? How do they move to the cash or checkout?

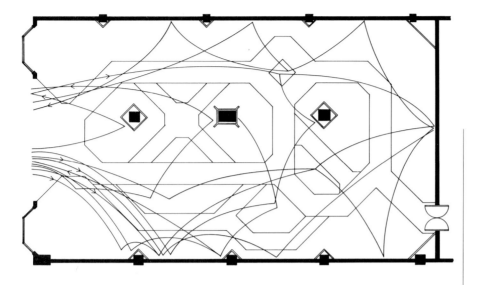

7.1

Tracking Plan. The above developmental plan shows how to track customer movement. Note that 4 of 6 entrants first move to the right. Hot spots and areas for impulse items can be detected.

TRACKING PLAN

A tracking plan is a simulated plan with symbols to use for following customers' movements. A few random samples of shoppers noted on duplicate plans can show a pattern. Some stores studied customer flow in their stores and responded by repositioning departments. They overlapped the patterns of entry and saw where their customers tended to move, touch merchandise, pick up, and buy.

These sheets with plotted patterns should be kept to use as reference when thinking about the design of the new space, as well as adjusting the stock content by area, so that *the merchandise that the merchant wants the customer to see first is in the prime position.*

These studies can also be done with time-lapse photography. Time-lapse is a technique in which a camera is mounted in a fixed position, focused on an area, and timed to take an exposure every 15 or 30 seconds.

In playback, the action of the entire day can be condensed to about 15 minutes.

Now return to the department or area manager and get specific. Ask:

- *Are there any places on the floor that can be called "hot spots"? These are places that get the most customer attention regardless of the merchandise.*
- *What are their best selling items?*
- *Are there out-of-stock situations? (Check the best sellers first.)*
- *Is there room for more stock?*
- *Who are the competitors?*
- *Is sales-service a needed implement for this product?*
- *Do the customers look for manufacturer's labels?*

Answers at this stage are a combination of real reactions and attitudes. They are governed by the respondents history, aspirations, biases, company loyalty, and their own treatment by their superiors.

DEFINING THE DEPARTMENT'S ROLE

Once you have collated the numerical, the subjective, and the observed information you can then start to define the roll that the department can play in the spectrum of the company sales. *As a designer, your per-*

spective is broad, fresh, and hopefully unbiased. The main purpose of all of this previous exploration is to make the designer think like a merchant, and see like a customer!

From here on in the planning process, I have found how consistently easy and logical the final plan turns out. *It is as if the designer's hand is guided by the merchant's eye.* The flexibility in this planning process comes from the specifics of each merchandise sub-classification.

THE RESULTING PLAN

Designers can now present a plan or a layout that shows where customers are most likely to see and go, in accord with the physical placement in the area. The fixturing then corresponds to the item quantity needed, and the possible sales maintenance. We can evaluate sales by item, by department, in a planned sequence of cause and effect.

Now the designer can sit at the drafting table, no longer isolated from the real situation, *but in command, visually and verbally, of the merchandise category.* The knowledge of why the merchandise was bought, how it sells, and the customers in that market permits the creative efforts to flow within a parameter of logic that unifies the store's mission to the image presented at point-of-purchase.

If the project calls for a gutting of the area, the design preparation process is the same. Should the project be less capital intensive, the positions of the curtain (non-supporting) walls, the hard (fixed) aisles, and the entry points, will probably not change. In a department change, the adjacencies and the inter-departmental flow remain the same.

The basic merchandise plan is roughed in. The placement of the various categories is visualized from a combination of the walking tour, the prime merchandise, and the assimilation of virtually all the previously gathered information. This sorting out of the details is as exciting aesthetically and as creatively stimulating as selecting the finishes.

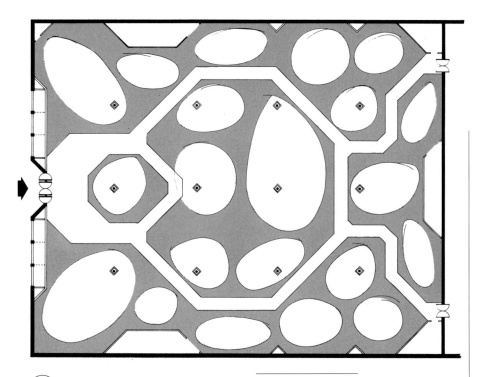

7.2

Bubble Plan. Once a primary aisle plan is developed and the merchants have declared their merchandise thrust, designers can quickly outline general area sizes and adjacencies that will in most instances serve to contain the items in each subdivision of each category.

ADD THE MERCHANDISE

Label areas by merchandise and sketch a bubble around each name. Try to maintain the proportion of each bubble to the importance of the item by its previous placement, and its discussed potential. *Does the plan make aesthetic sense as well as merchandising sense?*

Darken the areas between the bubbles. They generally should fall out where you have placed the aisles. If not, move the aisles; after all, it is only pencil. The plan at this stage is called a *bubble, or potato plan.* Check the merchandise categories to see if they can all live in the space.

How many points of interest have been created, and how many architechtural positions can you make as theatrical as possible?

Once satisfied that the plan can hold

the merchandise, and that there is flow into and out of the area, and that you can visualize the presentation, you are at the point of selecting fixtures and housing that determine self- or sales-service. You move from the overhead square foot view of the plan to sculptural cubic foot considerations. Columns and walls become part of the fixturing. Fitting rooms, stock rooms, and offices are placed for staff or customer facility, as well as creating wall surface position.

Start to visualize the department in a proportionate, sculptural balance of sections that fit within the whole. It should reflect a visual bulk with a consistency to product adjacencies.

ADD THE LIGHTING

Next, place the lighting positions. Indicate general ambient illumination, with positions for flexible highlighting in the department and on the aisles. Perimeter, or side lighting positions, should be considered. Most stores, including specialty stores, have the worst potential for proper lighting at the front of the store and departments. (See Chapter 14.)

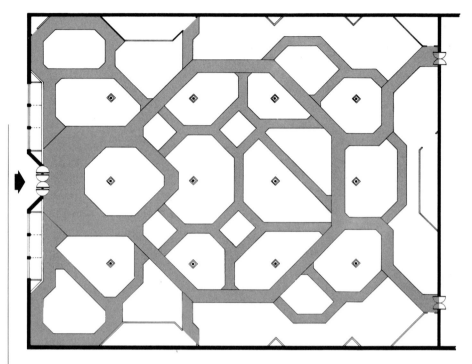

CHARTING THE PATHWAYS

Each area of the store and department has an innate traffic flow. Regardless of the merchandise, there is always a potential path that customers will take to and into a department. My preference is to determine the position that the customers first see in the department. That place is generally on the main aisle. That aisle position I reserve for the most important issue of the moment—a display or merchandise presentation that is the *feature presentation.*

Vertical merchandising means front-to-back as well as up-and-down. Relating items in a sequence from the first aisle point to the focal point on the wall makes the assortment easier to read.

The second area for consideration is a place on the wall or the column directly behind, in a vertical line from the feature presentation. This place I call the *focal point,* and will hold the bulk of the stock represented in the feature presentation.

As these two points are laid out, plan a pathway that leads from the feature on the aisle to the focal point on the wall. Sketch in aisles that move customers from the main traffic aisle to the focal point. These aisles are *secondary aisles.* They will be formed by fixture placement as the rest of the area takes shape.

The plan can start to develop an *internal aisle pattern.* The necessity for moving customers in and around the stock becomes a practical consideration of reaching all the needed categories. In virtually all instances of remerchandising, the previous balance of stock to space has to be considered first. In the sample plan shown, it looks as if there are too many aisles, and that the merchandise will not fit. In every situation where merchandise has been previously placed in a grid pattern arrangement, the *diagonal aisle system,* with proper use of the wall, has held more stock than before, sometimes as much as 100 percent more. The merchandise areas remaining permit a grouping or chunking of each category. In practice, if the merchandise does not fit the space, reconfigure the internal aisles by realigning the fixtures.

7.3

Prime and secondary traffic aisle. The aisles conform to a combination of the merchandise bubble plan and the bounce plan.

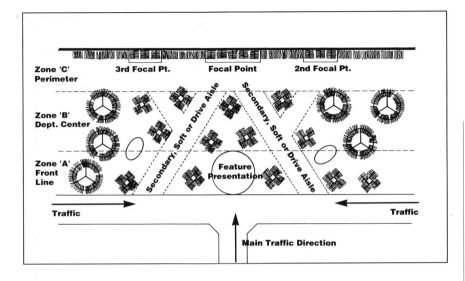

Zone 'C'
Perimeter   3rd Focal Pt.   Focal Point   2nd Focal Pt.

Secondary, Soft or Drive Aisle

Zone 'B'
Dept. Center

Secondary, Soft or Drive Aisle

Zone 'A'
Front
Line

Feature
Presentation

Traffic →   ← Traffic

↑ Main Traffic Direction

(7.4)

**Department Layout. This plan
also shows a tight clustering of
fixtures. Customers do not like to
shop when the space is too open.
Note that the fixtures are grouped
according to sight lines, and are
not on a grid pattern.**

DESIGN FOR SUCCESS

Decor selection or design features is an interpretation of the earlier information gathering. The designer's comprehension of the entire merchandising process, image message, and corporate mission is assisted, not overwhelmed, by aesthetics. The clarity of the presentation is the most important issue.

A successful store design represents the designer's integrity in being true to the client's corporate public identity. It should not be memorable just for the architecture, or the amusing decorative details. If the area sells, it is good design.

Successful designs allow the goods to flow, the department to breathe, and the customers to shop.

Chapter Eight

Promotions and Seasonal Decor

here is a yearly cycle to merchandising. Retailers base their plans on monthly themes that repeat from year to year, almost without exception. Each theme represents an opportunity for the retailer to promote specific merchandise that relates to a time period when customers are more likely to buy certain items. Except in countries where climate or religious festivals make a standard calendar unique, monthly events are highly repetitive. Designers may resolve the continuing need for decor installation and lighting positions with permanent mounting positions for promotional material.

Month	Theme	Merchandise Suggestion
January	Sales / Clearance	White clearance /Promo
February	Holiday	Special purchase
March	Spring	Fashion / Home improvement
April	Easter	Children / Brides
May	Mother's Day	Jewelry / Intimate
June	Father's Day	Shirts / Ties
July	Sales / Clearance	All categories
August	Back-to-school	Children
September	Fall fashions	Women's RTW
October	Selected topic	Women's classical evening
November	Christmas	Total store
December	Christmas	Total store

(8.1)

Monthly Merchandising Themes and Suggested Merchandise.

MONTHLY MERCHANDISING THEMES

To accommodate the decor package for these monthly themes, the promotion design team will mount the decor on or in the facade of the store, the windows, the perimeter, ceiling, columns, and in center floor. These positions will require one or all of the following four items.

- *Electrical outlets (wall, floor, and ceiling)*
- *Bulb sockets*
- *Light track*
- *Hanger bolts or hooks*

It is far more cost-effective to install these items during construction of a new store or renovation of an existing space. The promotional effect can be augmented in a planned, sequential format that adds visual spice to existing decor. Examples abound where stores have used the same decor package in a classic, traditional Christmas theme. Combined with the standard classical decor are newly-purchased items that bring the theme a more contemporary look.

The effect of in-store promotion is measurable. It contributes heavily to the sale of short-lived fashion items and increases the potential sale of basics. (In chapter 19 the evaluation checklist is used to show the visual effect on sales.) It is axiomatic that there is a direct corollary between the visual excitement and clarity of assortment presentation in a store and its state of financial health.

Following are some situations that I have experienced in fixing promotional additions to the architecture of the store.

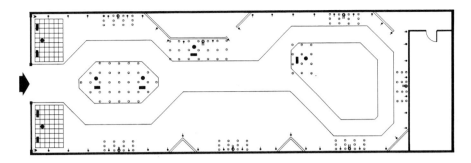

Plan promotion mounting positions with outlets and plugs.

By adhering to the sequence of placement, the positions for plugs and outlets can fit stores of all sizes

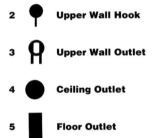

1 Ceiling Hook

2 Upper Wall Hook

3 Upper Wall Outlet

4 Ceiling Outlet

5 Floor Outlet

6 Vertical Wall Lighting Track

7 Ceiling Grid

8 Column with Fixture

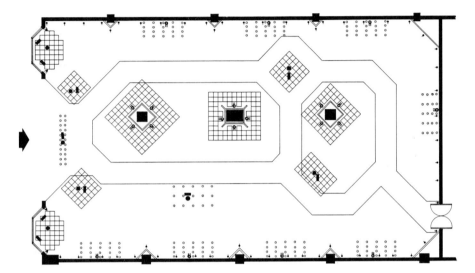

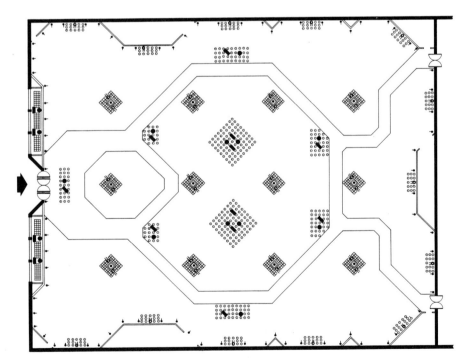

8.3

Building exteriors or interiors, trees, boats, bridges use light to accentuate the shape.

CHRISTMAS

The prime seasonal planning is for Christmas, regardless of the type or size of the store. The same proportion of flexibility required to show merchandise through the year is about the same degree of different positions used for Christmas decor. New locations will probably never exceed 10 percent of the fixed positions required for mounting, lighting, or electrifying material for a promotion.

The easiest way to achieve a Christmas look is to concentrate on two points.

1. Red: Used Everywhere but in France, where white, silver, and sometimes black are key Christmas colors. Printemps in Paris sets up a "Boutique Noire" every year.

2. Lights: Whether lights on strings, or candle-type fixtures are used, the profusion of the points of light adds to the festive feeling. There is no culture that disagrees with that premise.

To allow for the addition of these elements, the designer can provide receptacles for electrical items, and position hanging devices for signs and overhead trim. The former B. Altman's classically designed main store on Fifth Avenue in New York had simple, warm, additions of red on the main floor that gave it an immediate Christmas flavor. The store bought and kept in stock red lamp shades, red carpet, red panels, and red merchandise boxes to start their basic decor package. A change in the ribbons or foliage on the wreath was always calculated to work with the red background.

Any shape can be defined with lights. We can outline signs and buildings in lights, and trim outdoor trees in wraps of blinking lights.

Bonwit Teller, which like B. Altman's, closed in 1990, did a marvelous Christmas display on their main floor on Fifth Avenue. As a base for the Christmas trim, they used a spring theme trim that was installed in 1968. It became known as "The My Fair Lady Treatment," and lasted for many years after. It was an architectural treillage design, with creamy white lattice over a light-value grey wall. The Christmas ceiling trim of tulle, crystal stars, and string lights, without a major amount of red, played off the pastel treillage and created an ethereal heaven. Sadly, this trim was never repeated. The cost of mounting ceiling wire grids was so prohibitive that the man-hours used and the technical end of the installation cost much more than the materials.

For other monthly promotions, the placement of outlets, sockets, track, and mounting positions can be determined by examining the visual needs from major Christmas decor impact, area boutiques, and item signs. The effects created when great visual excitement combines with wonderfully desirable merchandise leads directly to an urgency to purchase.

SIGNS

Signs are a major part of the retail ethic. Signs are hung from the ceiling, are mounted on columns, can cover a window, are put in frames on a wall, and are dropped into a department and on the sides of the escalator. Without pre-installation planning, signs can detract from the visual ambiance of a selling space.

Design teams can initiate programs to control each sign for legibility and message while retaining the architectural integrity of the space. Following are suggestions for general signing.

- *Where positions are fixed, back lighting can be used. Self-contained back-lit directories should be placed in a sequence to reinforce directional movement, and can also be used singly for seasonal or sale messages. This requires a pattern of floor outlets.*
- *Mounting hooks can be placed in columns to accept banners or other hardware. Electrical outlets should be placed at the top and the bottom of each exposed column.*

- *The main aisle is the place where most promotions will occur. Its repetitive use and need for fast change requires adaptable lighting and mounting positions.*
- *Chapter 14, discusses the need for electrical and track positions in the window. Designers may also consider installing a supply closet in the window bank for ladder storage. A ceiling grid is a simple necessity. At the corner mullions, vertical strips of perforated library shelving provide useful loops to run invisible wire to support a mannequin, run strings of lights, etc.*

CLEARANCE SALES

This store-wide, semi-annual event is generally an aesthetic eyesore. Merchants should not have an area or the entire store lose its integrity. Heavy advertising draws increased traffic, and full-price merchandise moves as well as the sale items.

Customers expect some degree of difference in presentation, but not a disregard for the dignity of the store's image.

8.4

Eaton's, Canada. The open well in the escalator bank holds a multi-sided sign that is used as a directory and a sale banner.

(8.5)

Bloomingdale's, New York City. These shops are in areas that are changed yearly to coordinate with a storewide theme.

Sale merchandise presentation requires a different, but not out-of-character presentation. Some clutter is permitted because the appearance of hyper-value stimulates business.

Merchandise on sale should be located at the most propitious places in the store and in each department. Spotlights draw customers to dump tables or floor fixtures.

MAJOR THEME PROMOTIONS

Few stores currently commit to the merchandise expense of a theme promotion in October. Most opt to have an anniversary sale in a month that falls between the introduction of the year's biggest fashion line and the onset of the end-of-the-year holidays. About 30 years ago, department stores began to use this time to promote merchandise from specific countries around the world. Some also did U. S. themes, and others had catch-all international themes. The purpose was to use key spaces in the store to create the impression that a major part of the store's stock came from a defined geographic area.

Stores like Bloomingdale's carry on that tradition today. They use boutiques to put together a merchandise story, generally placed in a high traffic area. Food sampling and sales are an integral part of the presentation. If the sell-through is good, the shop is given an extended lease on its space and becomes a Christmas outpost. A series of promotions will use the same positions for decor and display in the same areas. They will need consistent hanging positions and electrical outlets. Available hardware positions will increase design options.

Other repetitive themes that require advance planning and product presence are home fashion shows, flower shows, white sales, and local tie-ins that get yearly attention.

It is still rare to see specially-bought, themed merchandise promoted in specialty stores used as a direct bridge to build Christmas, presented as promotions during October.

As shopping center developers are becoming more retail-oriented, some are using the common areas for seasonal decor packages. They promote themes and special merchandise by leasing carts, kiosks, and temporary stores to merchants with appropriate items (See Chapter 18). The continued use of the center court for this activity, other than fashion shows, makes it imperative that the designers of shopping centers, enclosed or strip, provide the technical support needed to quickly mount theatrical, seasonal, and in these spaces, large scale decor. The need for mounting positions in common areas is the same as the requirements for stores in the center.

Chapter Nine

The Basis For Fixture Selection

Designers need to consider the whole store as a merchandising tool. Fixture choice complements the fixed architectural design after it first properly complements the merchandise assortment. Fixture selection is an integral contributor to the visual image of the store.

The assessment of the merchandising needs and the continuing staff maintenance designates the initial factors of fixture choice. There is an inherent style and design finesse called for in the selection.

Choosing fixtures for a department is not just a matter of placing a group of circles and squares on a plan. Throughout the entire design process, the merchant's goal of assortment clarity must be kept in mind. At the conclusion of this chapter, there is a chart that suggests a match-up between fixtures and merchandise for full-margin and sale times.

9.1

A. Shorts on a rounder. Invariably this fixture will always produce this result. Cubic area is totally misused.

B. Boxes on glass shelves. The markdowns will drop even further as customers refuse to buy from this anti-aesthetic presentation.

The issues of maintenance, cycles of change, and exclusivity are factors in fixture selection. The following list, arranged by most to lesser importance, sets priorities for most fixture selection.

- *Merchandise*
- *Sales-service, or self-service*
- *Sequence of stock flow*
- *Exclusivity, price points of merchandise*
- *Stock arrival schedule or rotation*
- *Quantity on-hand and customer flow*
- *Department depth*
- *Standard, mass produced, or custom built*
- *Budget*
- *Aisles and sub-categories*
- *Flexibility and floor fixtures on wheels*
- *Display and signing*
- *Rolling racks for transport*
- *Manufacturers' and designer fixtures*

MERCHANDISE

All merchandising starts with merchandise.

It seems obvious, but it is not always the way the work is approached. A good look at the merchandise should show the store designer more than style. It determines and narrows the choice of fixtures.

An important element in all fixtures used for RTW and shelving is height. Most available fixtures are vertically adjustable for any garment. When considering a unit that holds robes, dresses, coats, or any long hanging item, the items should be off the floor and still be at reasonable eye level for viewing and selection. Jackets, pants, and shirts may be single-hung on a bar. Sometimes they could be shown one above the other by using adapters.

Most of the difficulty comes when selecting fixtures for small items, such as children's, lingerie, or departments that have seasonal needs for shorts, swimwear, or crop tops. Often the fixture chosen, either by the designer or by the staff, shows too much space under the garment so that an empty space that is greater than the bulk of the merchandise is created. When there is more air space under the merchandise than the space occupied by the visual bulk of the stock, the negative space captures the customer's attention.

Shelf merchandise uses the same principle. However, since shelf merchandise is stacked from the bottom to the top, the space above the merchandise on the shelf is the negative. The selection of box sizes, more than flat folded merchandise, determines the placement of the second, third, and fourth shelves. When products come in packages of different sizes, vertical relation from shelf to shelf is still important. Flat folded RTW can be adjusted in stacks to prefixed shelf heights.

Solutions to these problems combine fixture adaptability, careful selection, and some customizing.

SALES-SERVICE OR SELF-SERVICE

When the store's management firmly believes in sales-service, the designer must follow this principle through the entire shopping process. Most stores oriented to sales-service encourage some degree of self-selection. If merchandise is going to be shown in any depth, customers should be permitted time to settle into an area of merchandise where they feel comfortable and ready to make a purchase. At one time, store personnel brought selected garments from a back room to customers who were seated on a charming settee in the department or fitting room. Today, there is probably only one type of sale that is made that way: precious gems.

Most stores today depend on the customer to walk into the store, around, in and through several departments. Shoppers can see many desirable items, enticingly presented, prior to making a single or multiple purchase. The fixtures used for presentation are known as "silent

salesmen." In fact, in several stores that have made their reputation on the sales-service concept, the staff spends more time maintaining the floor fixtures than the personnel of stores that are self-service. Even in stores that augment the salary of their staff with commissions, sales associates understand that overall presentation will increase their earnings.

The fixtures chosen for some self-selection must then permit a unit to be shown with a second or third item for coordination, or for comparison. *Groups of fixtures must therefore show a selection of the assortment that expresses the balance of sales personnel-to-service. Customers will get the implied message.*

The only fixture that demands absolute service is the counter, or case. For every bank of counters there must be at least one person to serve. Fragrance companies generally co-op the cost of sales personnel. Rarely are cosmetic or fragrance counters unattended. Staff shortages at counters are generally in departments that are fully owned and

COORDINATE GROUP STOCK MOVEMENT

	0-20 % - Poor Sellers		20-80% Average Sellers * (Basics)		80-100% Best Sellers	
Weeks	Sales-To-Stock Ratio	Fixture	Sales-To-Stock Ratio	Fixture	Sales-To-Stock Ratio	Fixture
1st	5%	Four-Way	10-15%	Four-Way	20-35%	Four-Way
2nd	5% Move Fixture Position	Four-Way	10-15%	Four-Way	20-25%	Four-Way
3rd	20% First Markdown Mid Dept. Position	Four-Way	10% Regroup with Basics	Four-Way	10% Re-Coordinate with Best Sellers	Four-Way
4th	Rearrange by End Use Category-Size First	Rounder	10%	Four-Way	15%	Four-Way
5th, 6th	Second Markdown	Rounder	5% Regroup by Color/Style	Rounder	Re-Coordinate by Color/Style	Rounder
7th, 8th	Combine All Broken Sizes on Different Rounders by Size for First or Final Markdowns					
12-14th	Clearance					

* Basics Are Average Sellers But Rarely Change Fixtures or Get Marked Down

9.3

Weekly Action Taken–Fixtures Used. This chart shows what is normal in most selling cycles for merchandise in a department. The types of fixtures that are my choice to help define the current salability are included.

controlled by the store. Small items that are theft-prone are placed in counter and wall cases and require sales assistance. Merchants should not forget that before going to the expense of building the counter and stocking it with costly inventory, it must be efficiently serviced.

SEQUENCE OF STOCK MOVEMENT

Picture-perfect stores look good in design magazines, but may be terrible for business. Every store needs flow and purchases, which lead to a "breathing" and a churning of the departmental space. An amount of expansion and contraction can be planned for initially, and then adjusted by the staff as the actual sales and stock replacement take place. *It is the imperfect store, handled with taste and charm, that creates the unique desire to shop with urgency.*

As sales of items continue, the merchandise starts to break in size range. In fashion stores, this is the constant result of keeping current.

The key to presenting fashion clothing is linked to the art of merchandising broken sizes. When the original seasonal assortment starts to sell, and new groups come in to refill the space, there must be a variety of fixtures and department areas to properly show the new groups as well as last week's best sellers. Here are the three basic selling velocities.

- *The best sellers, or about 10-20 percent of any normal assortment, will check out at a rate of 35-50 percent in the first*

week. By the end of the second week, there is usually less than one-half of the original group, often with one or more sizes missing.

- **The moderate sellers, or about 60 to 80 percent of the assortment.** These should sell at a rate of 15-25 percent in the first week, and be in broken sizes within three weeks to a month.

- **The third group are the worst sellers, or 'dogs.'** If there is a poor selling group, change the location first then change the fixture. They can be marked-down in season within two weeks of their first presentation. (Possibly only one normal Saturday is all that is needed to see the movement.) It may also be necessary to change the fixture to adjust the visual perception.

PRICE AND EXCLUSIVITY

Customers get their first idea of the store's price points by sighting the proportion of merchandise to the space. The first glimpse will cover the vertical and horizontal density, and the second will be the judgment of depth of either the space or the amount of repeat items on each fixture. A fixture may hold only one garment and still look complete, depending on the capacity of that fix-

ture. The customer gets the clear signal that they will get waited on, and probably get a fresh item from stock, because the single piece is a display or a demonstrator item. *But, leave a single garment on a fixture that was designed to hold a full size range, and both the sale and the credibility of the store are lost.*

Consider the opposite desired effect, where larger quantities of goods reflect a price-conscious purchase. Exclusivity is not the important factor, *unit quantity* is.

9.4

Before and after, four-way. The left photo shows a fixture that holds merchandise in broken sizes. It is put together poorly. The after photo has the same merchandise rearranged. The skirts which were on the waterfall front arm were moved to a side arm, opposite the skirts. Rule one of fixtures should be that bottoms are never shown on a slant arm. The repetition of the hangers makes them more visually exciting than the merchandise. The back arm was raised to show the front of the forward garment above the bottoms. There is a rhythm to the placement that conceals the fact that there are broken sizes.

DISTRIBUTION AND ROTATION

The speed at which merchandise arrives and is sold depends on several variables. The greatest variable is the ability of the staff to handle the flow of merchandise. Another important variable is the item count in each category that determines the fixture to be used. Item count and personnel ability is then factored by the cubic space and the speed of sales.

It is important to know whether the products come directly from the manufacturer, or whether they are first sent to a company warehouse for post-distribution. If they come from the manufacturer, many merchandise collections must be assembled in the store. If the merchandise is warehoused, then entire large groups can arrive in one shipment, including filler stock for replacement items. A variety of adaptable fixtures must be available for showing groups of like items that can then be regrouped to show coordinating merchandise.

NEW TYPE OF RETAIL

Off-price and warehouse club stores buy huge lots of specially ordered items or manufacturer's close-outs, or the stocks of bankrupt stores. In either case, quantities of goods hit the sales floor at one time, and remain until they sell down, and a new load comes in. Warehouse clubs have taken over the function of the jobber as some retailers will buy from the odd-lots of these stores and resell the merchandise.

Stock movement is volatile. Swings of inventory content can be made easier by having a combination of bulk and feature-type fixtures. In addition to the stocking of the fixtures, designers must provide space for erratic high/low customer flow. A store's profitabilty can depend on selling many items at relatively low margins to make up in volume what is lost in margin.

Warehouse-type stores with heavy traffic require more open space around the cash registers than stores with standard merchandise policies. Shopping carts and the rolling pallets require more maneuverability.

QUANTITY AND CUSTOMER FLOW

Even within the same chain, depending on location, you can expect varieties of customer count.

Center city stores will have more foot traffic than shops in any other location. The percentage of those who enter will be minor compared to other stores, but the actual numbers will be higher.

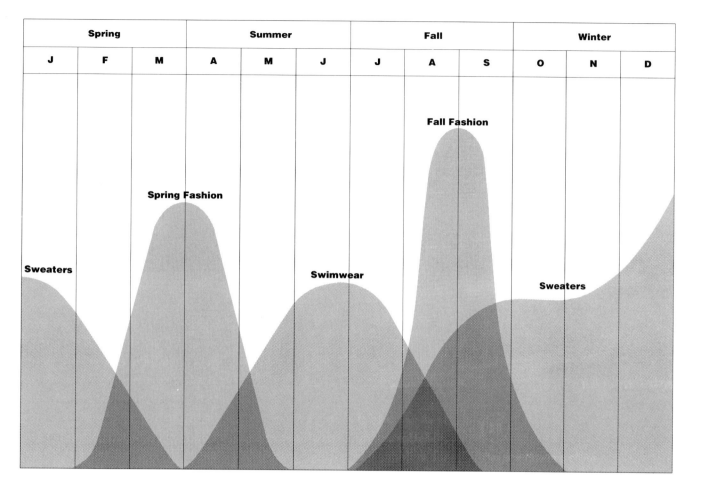

Spring			Summer			Fall			Winter		
J	F	M	A	M	J	J	A	S	O	N	D

Fall Fashion

Spring Fashion

Sweaters

Swimwear

Sweaters

Commuters sometimes use stores as passageways. The unexpected always happens in these stores. Items that would be in smaller supply in other locations require bulk presentation, although not with a warehouse look.

Customer action is faster, and shifts in attitude occur rapidly as goods arrive, or as customers gather around a fixture housing a good buy. The excitement and enthusiasm becomes contagious, encouraging additional shoppers who want to see what is for sale.

Mall stores of all sizes operate under the aegis of the mall. The developer creates a new mall entity that supports, and in turn is supported by, all the shops in the center. Few of these shops can be classified as destination locations, so they rely on the collective strength of the mall to bring in customer.

When evaluating the potential customer base, each mall must be judged independently. The designer must look at the mall's traffic, rather than the individual unit, to judge the true available customer potential.

Free-standing stores or stores in a strip mall will have a mix of customers that range from destination shoppers to casual browsers. They can be affected more severely by residential and commercial development as well as other demographic shifts. Shopping patterns are generally repetitive, and the store's staff tends to remain with the company longer. Each store needs fixture flexibility, but not as much as any of the other previously mentioned types.

9.5

Ready-to-Wear Merchandise Flow Chart. This chart presents information on the entry, rise, and decline of blocks of merchandise within a major category. The same type of flow chart can be constructed for subdivisions of each category.

(9.6)

Bermans, Minneapolis. The wall presentations were very clear, leaving the center to tell a third merchandise story. The group holds its space by layering the levels of the fixtures to create a low pyramid. This assists in sculpting the space, rather than having a flat and uninteresting space in the center of the floor.

DEPARTMENT DEPTH

Department depth in stores may be adjusted by aisle placement. In most stores, the wall is set back at least two fixtures from the main aisle or secondary aisle. As customers penetrate and shop the department wall, they then turn and exit, seeing items on the back side of the floor fixtures. With deep spaces that can hold three to seven fixtures in a line before reaching the wall, other intermediate floor groupings must be made.

Merchandise groups can be shaped into islands or clusters. In an island group, the fixtures nearer the main aisle can be the lead-in to a merchandise sub-division. A cluster should use fixtures for feature and bulking within each group. In effect, it becomes a small complete merchandise statement.

In stores that have controlled the department depth to a distance of 20 to 30 feet, designers must consider different purposes for the front line. The front holds most of the new stock that feeds visually to the feature presentation, which in turn leads the eye to the wall behind. The flexibility of height and positioning is needed more here because of the planned faster rotation of the merchandise.

In the center of the department or Zone B, the fixtures hold items for several purposes.

- *Maintaining seasonal basics.* In a RTW department, this item could be blazer jackets. In a hard goods department, the item could be cooking implements.
- *Recoordinating merchandise of broken sizes that has just passed its prime selling time.*
- *Groups of marked-down items, or unadvertised specials.*

In each instance the fixture and the merchandise must coordinate with the fixture in front, and finally lead the eye to the wall behind.

MANUFACTURERS STANDARD FIXTURES AND CUSTOM DESIGNS

Most store fixture needs can be met by the current assortments of fixture suppliers. In up-market stores, man-

agement and the designer may wish to have a totally unique fixture to visually state something about the dedication to luxury and exclusivity. *The image of the store, however, is based first on total merchandise presentation—not the fixtures alone.*

Fixture manufacturers specialize in different materials and different finishes. The choice of one or the other is possibly the only major distinction that can be made on a purely aesthetic basis. The danger of selecting different types of fixtures from two or more manufacturers for presentation in adjacent departments means that in time the fixtures will be mixed by some untrained staff member.

In some shops or departments, the merchandising units are part of the architecture (built-in fixtures). These fixtures generally hold a specific item. The control of the manufacturing and the packaging of that item can make these stores unique. Designers, in respecting the format of a pre-packaged store, must first meet the needs of the minimum basic assortment. In these stores the entire system is custom made.

BUDGET

There is one major criteria that should affect the total cost of the fixturing system: *durability*. When a fixture plan is prepared, virtually every merchandise need can be met with a standard budget. Even boutique-type presentations within a category can be found in the catalogue of pre-existing fixtures. If there is need to use special fixtures, most manufacturers would willingly furnish the user with manuals or photos of the unit in different presentation modes, and possibly give a seminar to the selling staff on the proper use and care of their fixtures.

The most expensive fixtures are counter cases. Most stores build these units to meet specifications. Electrical requirements, locking devices, drawers, and custom finishing make these units costly.

(9.7)

Body Shop, England. The sophistication of the material usage, the design, the color, and the technical brilliance of the mechanics of this chain make each shop responsive to the overall corporate message. Merchandising does not have to be in conflict with the environment.

Units. The shop design, merchandise delivery system, and the packaging had to be created as a whole.

9.8

In certain
environments a
compacting of
merchandise
works well. It gives
an idea of the
coordinate
possibilities in an
anatomically
correct relationship.

AISLES

The division of a store or a department is made to create a unity and an adjacency flow. The fixtures that are chosen for each merchandise category should not only be thought of as relating to the merchandise within that group, but also *how they relate to the transition from one area to another.*

It is possible to position a gift or a home fashion department next to a RTW department and still have reasonable relationships between the two merchandise groups. The aisles mark the point where the fixture and the merchandise must make the transition to a new group. A sensitivity to fixturing is needed in selection to decide scale, capacity, finish, and use.

FLEXIBILITY

At one time, fixture manufacturers sold fixtures based on the idea that flexibility was the key to its use. To achieve total flexibility, entire floors and ceilings were fitted with plugs for pole systems that could change walls into shelves, face-out hanging into shoulder hang, insert graphics and photos, and be the panacea for all merchandise problems. Flexibility, however, is costly when not absolutely necessary. Even well-executed departments such as the former BG shop in Bergdorf Goodman rarely used the total flexibility built into the system.

The degree of fixture flexibility actually needed for most continuing departments may amount to 10 percent of the total fixture assortment. Height variation in merchandise is hardly every accounted for, even though every fixture has a height adaptability. If a fixture is used for a long garment, and is then used for a short item, the space between the bottom of the item and the floor is often too great, creating negative space.

Some RTW fixtures have telescope arms that can add capacity or fit bulkier items more comfortably. Shelf depth is also adjustable when different shelves are used to fit larger or smaller packages. Merchandise depth in all categories must be dealt with on an ad hoc basis by a trained, motivated, sophisticated staff. Adapter arms that can be added to the uprights of most four-arm and 'T' stand fixtures should be standard equipment in departments that carry small merchandise and should also be available for all RTW departments. A vertical presentation of a top over a bottom brings a faster recognition to style selection than items hanging side by side.

PRODUCT DISPLAY AND SIGNING

Every fixture should contain a provision for signing. Few things disturb the integrity of the fixture presentation more than a sign which does not fit. Fixture signs are a necessity. Initial considerations include the amount of hardware and cost, with sufficient space to give information or price.

Merchandise units in RTW and home fashion can be used to make a display presentation. Round racks have center glass supports and four-arm units have space for a center plate. Others that do not provide this should be chosen judiciously because the end result of the presentation can become flat and dull.

Variety in merchandising techniques lets the eye ripple across the tops of the fixtures, stopping at a presentation of each front garment, display, or sign. Do not worry that you are unable to see over every fixture. Remember that customers do not stand still so their vision will not be blocked for very long. However, do not create a "wall" of fixtures. In most spaces, *a "wall" can be about six feet in length or anything that customers cannot see over or get around by taking one step in either direction.*

ROLLING RACKS

These workhorses that are used to transport merchandise from the loading dock to the sales floor can have another, more purposeful use. Have you ever witnessed the activity around a rack that is moving to a department? Customers gravitate to it as a salesperson starts to transfer merchandise from a rolling rack to a floor fixture.

(9.9)

Saks 5th Avenue, New York City. Only the price tags say sale. The fixture does the rest of the work.

Fixture	Merchandise	Use For Sale
T-Stand	Long Items and New Merchandise	No
Three Arm	Long Items and New Merchandise	No
Four Arm	All RTW Except Long Items	Markdowns and Special Purchase
Multiple Arm 5 & More	Try To Avoid	Try To Avoid
Spiral Waterfall	Try To Avoid	Try To Avoid
Half Round	Try To Avoid	Try To Avoid
Rounder	Single Categories with Full Mark On	OK, But Sized
Three Level Rounder	Coordinates Or 3 Styles Same Fabric	OK
Straight or H or X	Single Categories with Full Mark On	OK, But Sized
Cubes	Accessories & Folded & Packaged	No
Shelves	Folded & Packaged	Yes
Wall	Folded & Packaged	Yes, But Last Choice
Tables	Folded & Packaged	No
Promo Tables	Packaged & Bulk	Yes

Fixture List

MANUFACTURER FIXTURES

This topic stirs strong sentiments on the part of the manufacturer and retailers. Manufacturers feel that their merchandise should be distinguished from the merchandise of other manufacturers in the category. Many, such as Polo, Levi, Lauder, Liz Claiborne, Esprit, etc., would not consider placing their merchandise in the store without strict coordination and control.

Some stores have specific rules not to let manufacturers' fixtures into the stores. Others permit them in with the proviso that they are approved by the planning or the visual department. Still others employ no policy, and the divisional merchant or the buyer makes the decision.

The obvious problems for retailers are that the fixture is designed to set the manufacturer's group aside from the rest of the merchandise, and must have special attention given to the merchandise movement. The problem for the manufacturer is that retailers do not obligate themselves to restock the fixture with the merchandise from that supplier. In either case, the end result is often a poor representation to the shopper.

Some manufacturers supply and maintain a special fixture grouping or boutique. *This creates an exclusivity factor that guarantees the troubled retailer that its nearby competition will have the same, easily identifiable presentation unit.*

A third way that the manufacturer and the store will benefit from a program of "package buying" is when the supplier co-ops or partially funds the presentation devices for their merchandise in a department. The suppliers' needs are met with the planning done by the store's personnel. In all cases, the fixture should not represent a Trojan Horse, a gift that does more for the giver than for the recipient.

Chapter Ten

Ready-to-Wear

very product has a priority in the mind of the customer. The sequence of product selection changes from item to item. Seasonal desirability of the product will temporarily alter that sequence. The fluidity needed to accommodate these changes can be met by the designer. Retail store design starts by understanding the product.

Individual products have a pre-established basis for selection. By understanding these customer preferences, and by providing equipment and the atmosphere to aid in the presentation, designers can assist in increasing unit sales. The following chart lists most ready-to-wear products with suggested customer priority. *The sequence of selection by the customer must be mirrored in the sequence of product presentation.*

PRODUCT PRIORITY

Product	1	2	3	4
Appliances (large)	Brand	Price	End use	Color
Appliances (small)	Brand	Design	Price	
Bags	Style	Material	Price	
Bedding	Size	Pattern/Color	Price	
Blouses (Junior)	Style	Color	Price	
Blouses (Women)	Color	Style/Fabric	Size	Price
Bras	Construction	Manufacture's Name	Size	
Camisoles	Color	Fabric	Style	Price
China (Casual)	Pattern/Color	Price	Properties	
China (Fine)	Brand	Pattern/Design	Price	
Coats (Adult)	Color	Style/Fabric	Price	Weight
Coats (Children)	Size	Price	Style	Color
Cookware	Brand/Color	Price	End use	
Cosmetics	Brand	Color	Price	
Dresses				
New stock	Color	Style	Size	Price
Old stock	Size	Color/Style	Price	
Gifts Home (Christmas)	End use	Price	Brand	
Gifts Home (General)	Room	Material	Color	Price
Glass (Houseware)	Shape	Price		
Glass (Stemware)	Style	Brand	Price	
Hardware/Tools	Brand name	Usage	Price	
Hose (Men's)	Length/Brand	Size	Color	Price
Hose (Women's)	Brand	Color/Size	Price	
Jeans	Brand/Style/Fit	Price		
Jewelry (Fine)	End use	Price		
Linens (Table)	Size	Style	Color	Price
Panties	Fabric	Style	Color	Size
Pants (Men)	Size	Fabric	Color	Price
Perfume	Aroma	Brand	Price	
Scarves	Fabric	Price	Color	Pattern
Shirts (Men)	Size	Color	Style	Price
Shoes (Men)	Brand	Style	Color	Price
Shoes (Running)	Brand/Style	Soles	Comfort	Price
Shoes (Tennis)	Brand	Comfort	Price	
Shoes (Women)	Style	Color	Brand	Price
Socks (Athletic)	Texture/Fabric	Price		
Suits (Men)	Style	Fabric	Color	Price
Ties	Width/Design	Color	Fabric	Price
Towels	Color/Brand	Pile	Size	Price
Toys	Function	Brand	Price	
TV/Electronics	Brand	Price	Model	
Umbrellas (Men)	Handles	Price	Size	
Umbrellas (Women)	Color	Price	Size	
Watches	Price/Brand	Face	Banding	

Ready-to-wear (RTW) is first among all merchandise groups. From the time when fabric was sold to the home sewer, seamstress, or tailor, or in made-to-measure departments that were employed in stores, to today's couture and mass-made clothing, apparel has been the backbone of retail sales. *Stores that most clearly present the widest and freshest appearing stock are the ones that have the best potential to develop a strong market position.* Their selling ethic is represented by a staff that is trained to use the sales floor as a tool to best show management's intent in putting their assortment together.

Presentation must be cycled so that regular shoppers see a new presentation each time they visit the store. The consumer's frequency of visit must be equally matched by the same frequency of change, even if it is only the *appearance* of change.

The objective in RTW is to create an air of urgency to purchase when most of the merchandise is at full margin. *The proportion of the merchandise in depth, and in its relation to the entire group of merchandise in the area, determines the choice of equipment that designers can use to fixture the shop.* The designer's options are predetermined by the policy and the merchandise of each department. The main categories of women's, men's, children's, and lingerie must be approached individually.

The nuances of product price/value perception are best dealt with by using specific examples of merchandise that is the cornerstone of each category.

References will be made to departments by using the terms "areas," "shops," "stores," or "departments." Except for floor plan configurations, these terms are interchangeable.

WOMEN'S RTW

The most-bought item in women's clothing is the separate top. Year after year, this item will far out-pace the sales of bottoms, dresses, or coordinates. Whether the top is a blouse or a knit item, the width of selection, and the necessity to maintain year-round and seasonal basics, as well as short-term fashion items, provides the designer with the most direct cues to establish the core of the presentation, and the presence of the store in its market.

10.1

Product Priority Chart

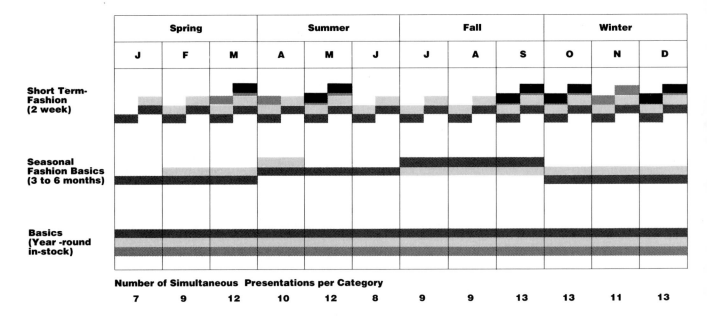

	Spring			Summer			Fall			Winter		
	J	**F**	**M**	**A**	**M**	**J**	**J**	**A**	**S**	**O**	**N**	**D**
Short Term-Fashion (2 week)												
Seasonal Fashion Basics (3 to 6 months)												
Basics (Year-round in-stock)												

Number of Simultaneous Presentations per Category

7	**9**	**12**	**10**	**12**	**8**	**9**	**9**	**13**	**13**	**11**	**13**

(10.2)

Fashion Change Chart

Figure 10-2 is a practical way to look at the flow of merchandise during a year. This chart applies to virtually all categories of merchandise, with some shifts due to seasonal adjustments and promotional needs. In the majority of all merchandise groups in all types of stores, 80 percent of any assortment is *basic*. It is the bread-and-butter of a group, and must be kept in stock, whether it be a year-round basic, or a shorter term item.

Short-term fashion items give more visual spice to the assortment. However, these items are the most volatile of the group, and may sell out the day that they are placed on the floor, or in the case of "hot" novelty items, may sell even before they are unpacked. They are also the items that will be marked down first when they do not sell well.

Fashion items are about 20 percent of the entire group, but may comprise 40 to 60 percent of total volume. These items turn faster than

basics, and sell more items in each square foot per year. Edward Finkelstein, president of Macy's said, "You can never predict the velocity of sales of a best selling item." *In designing the selling space, the designer's main task is to permit the customer to be aware of the presence of the basic items, feature the newer, more volatile fashion items, and permit sale reduced items to be seen in the same area.*

WALL PRESENTATION

The wall is the starting point for departmental design, and is the designer's primary concern. Women's merchandise is generally placed on 18"-wide hangers. Vertical key strip standards set into the wall should be 22" on center. This will permit the women's merchandise, except for outer wear, to be faced-out without a large amount of wall space between garments. If the merchandise is to be shoulder hung, then the difference of placement will hardly show.

Many designers simply place the vertical key strips at 24" on center positions. Sometimes this is done to screw the vertical strip directly into the wall studding. The extra distance between the face-out hanging garments creates a void that becomes a pattern in itself which detracts from the merchandise.

Face-out hardware is available to set the merchandise at any reachable height without the use of brackets, bars, and adaptors. Even though the hardware in general usage today is well-made and well-designed, too much becomes a distraction from the presentation. The less hardware that shows, the better, and it is also less costly.

The position of the wall in relation to the main traffic pattern can determine the size and configuration of the department. Wall fixturing should provide the maximum flexibility for the four methods used to present stock: *face-out, shoulder hang, folded, and rolled.*

The combined use of these techniques can be the visual signature of the store. A clearly presented assortment on the wall also acts as the merchandise sign of the department.

Changes in inventory level, garment fabrication, and style make it imperative to let the wall accept all arrangements and quantities of stock of the most desired and desirable merchandise.

First consider a position for the basics, and then the placement of the fashion items. The true merchant glamourizes the basic presentation without giving it the prime position. Customers must see the basic assortment and recognize that the items will still be in stock when they finish their browsing through the department and the store.

Shoppers who come to a store for a particular item are called "destination shoppers." They generally come to buy a basic item, or for a current seasonal or advertised sale item.

Designers provide positions that allow for the stocking and presenting of large quantities of basic merchandise in a manner that fits the company's visual image, and also fulfills the very critical need of stocking and service.

Here the information from the initial interview process gets interpreted into practical terms. If the store is committed to sales-service, the designer has the latitude to use shelving for folded garments. The care of a shelved unit creates the need for constant personnel attention. Most customers tend to refold and replace an item on a shelf if all the rest of the items are so kept. But, have one garment where the arms are falling off the shelf, or the item is replaced by just stuffing it back onto the shelf, and the fixture will soon become an anti-aesthetic avalanche.

The advantage of shelved merchandise is that a larger quantity of items can be held in the same cubic area than hung items. The increase is approximately three to six times, depending on the fiber in the garment. Folded merchandise on a shelf or a table signifies to customers that the store offers sales-service.

The wall position for the placement of stock should be arranged so that the range of the primary merchandise can be shown. *A key location on the wall of a department is the first position that the customer sees when entering the area from the primary traffic pattern.* By following the course of movement from the entry of the store to the department, this point becomes evident. Designers should provide fixture positions at the perimeter that can take the key merchandise to the highest point on the wall, even only in display form.

With the prime fashion issues centered here, the staff can then be free to use other forms of presentation to make the rest of the assortment support that specific issue. The physical presence of the key item must provide a merchandising critical mass.

(10.3)

Top left : The attempt to evenly space the shelves does nothing to communicate the idea of fashion.

Top right : The prime attention is drawn away from the merchandise by the light splash on the wall.

Bottom left : Harry Rosen, Toronto. The fixture system, the finishes, the lighting, and the display relate to the specific quality of the merchandise.

Bottom right : It is still self-service because customers can reach all styles.

BASIC FIXTURES:

Four-arm multiple height. These fixtures can comfortably hold between 64 and 80 garments. That translates into two groups of tops and bottoms. Most buyers will try to put together a minimum group of four items in a full size range within a style group. Therefore, two four-arm fixtures with 16" arms may be used. I rarely recommend their use to show only four different bottoms within the same group. They can be used to show tops in a variety of ways: all wovens, all knits, or a combination of the two, if there is a logic to their coordination.

Round racks. With either one level ring, or with three sections, the adjustable height of round racks allows for a grouping of items that compare to the use of shoulder hang on the wall.

- *They can be used for new stock that shows the variety of colors available of a single garment.*
- *They can show garments of similar styles with the same fabrication.*
- *They are excellent for clearances, where the face of the garment might not be the selling factor.*

Size is the first thing that shoppers look for when purchasing sale merchandise. Clothing departments that lack large capacity racks put a heavy and unnecessary burden on the selling staff.

Three-arm racks. When merchandising a dress or an outerwear department, I find that three-arm fixtures serve better than four-arms. Customers may buy in different groups better suited to be shown in threes, but I believe that the real reason is the overall bulk that the single four-arm fixture gets when it is dressed out in long merchandise. It becomes unsightly and almost by itself makes a wall of stock.

Compare coats on a three-arm to a four-way, or a rounder full of dresses. In the latter two, the aesthetics of the

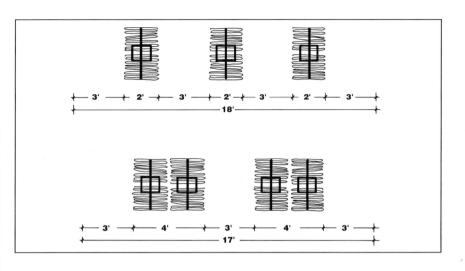

"T" stand diagram.
In one less foot of running space, an
additional T-stand is added, showing
24-36 more garments.

overall fixture become intrusive on the design of the items, and on the sensitivities of customers. Three-arm racks are less bulky in their ratio to floor space to merchandise unit count. They also can show bottoms, tops, and jackets in small easily identifiable groups.

"T" stands. Once thought of as the *sine qua non* of RTW areas, they now misrepresent the manner that most stores buy the merchandise. For the overwhelming majority of stores, larger groups of merchandise are set on the floor than can be housed comfortably on "T" stands. "T" stands are the first to show broken groups, and so require more care than given to other fixtures. They also use floor space incorrectly.

The best use for a "T" stand is in combination with one or two others. When placed side by side they hold the same quantity as a four-arm unit, without the space in the center of the four-arm. There would even be a small gain of total floor space used. In this configuration, they group well for the front line of most areas.

(10.5)

Nordstrom. These two presentations of men's shirts show two visually responsive, merchandise-sensitive assemblages of basic items with accessories and other coordinated basics.

categories. Some sort of display will always find its way on top, so provide lighting from above, or design self-contained illumination within the structure of the fixture.

According to Harry Rosen, CEO of the Canadian chain of the same name, folding pants on tables became a symbol of a new way of merchandising. His sales force felt that pants on tables would look like sale items. But Mr. Rosen persisted. He placed the pants on tables in neat piles, and proceeded to use fine displays of tops with them. The results of this "bold" move can still be seen today. "This is the only way to sell trousers," he said, and the sales force today echoes that thought.

Some women's stores are adapting the men's merchandising technique for folded pants on tables. As presentation techniques develop, table display has now become a major art using the combined skills of merchants and the visual merchandising team. Until recently, table merchandising was considered only for markdowns and dump merchandise.

Before you put a table on the plan, get the commitment from the people who will run the store that they will share the responsibility for the merchandise appearance at all times.

Etageres, tables, and center floor shelving units. For merchandise that comes pre-packaged, cube shelves of glass, or wood, are needed. Make sure that the shelf dividers are the specific width that permits one stack, or face-out, without falling over. Other packages should never be stuffed on the sides to keep the stack straight.

Sweater stacking is preferred over hanging knits. Hanger snag and stretching will quickly make a garment unattractive to customers. Because sweaters will change in weight seasonally, shelf heights and horizontal spacers should be adjustable.

The height of each center floor unit should not exceed 60", unless the purpose is to create a wall between areas that can become the transition bridge between two major

DEPARTMENT DEPTH

You can sell more merchandise to the same customer, in less time, and with the same assortment, if you permit and encourage department penetration. After all, if we can get customers to walk to the wall, when they turn around to exit they can see the remaining 50 percent of the assortment!

The depth that I recommend for most merchandise departments ranges between 20 to 30 feet from the main traffic aisle to the wall. Why not more? From the customer's point-of-view, it becomes too much of a commitment to enter and think of exiting. When entering an area customers must feel comfortable that leaving is just as easy. It becomes more than the space that is prohibitive. The total assortment reaching from the aisle to the wall becomes a mass of items that multiply the choices and the time that customers must spend to make intelligent buying decisions.

For a space that measures 50 feet wide by 25 feet deep, the fixtures can be arranged to show the merchandise, and the presentation is cycled to make a new look easily. Each sub-group can correspond to the promotional calendar, and not distort the fashion effect of the department.

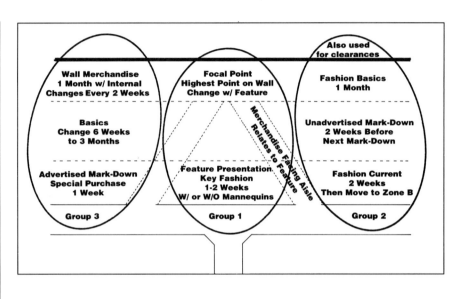

VERTICAL MOVEMENT

Vertical does not only mean up and down. It takes on a new significance when relating it to the plan. It starts to mean a line from front to back, a row of merchandise that coordinates from the front to the key position on the wall. The movement may flow from peaks to valleys, but always driving the eye to the place on the wall that we want customers to see.

AISLES

The need for passage is always developed from the objective to have shoppers walk in and around the department. Seeing customers shopping in one area always adds to the credibility of the merchandise and to other

10.6

Basic Departmental Layout. Within this format most merchandise categories can be placed. It is not necessary to follow the exact scheme, as long as there is a rational for the blocking. By maintaining the three key ideas of focal point, feature presentation, and secondary aisles, the setting of each sub-category will flow more easily.

(10.7)

Bradlees. The nearly even horizontal stripping between the merchandise and the wall creates a pattern that is stronger than any sub-group of items.

M Store, Montreal. An early version of vertical color striping and horizontal hip placement. The delicacy of the alternating colors helps to pick out different styles.

browsers. Internal, or secondary aisles, also help to "chunk" the total assortment.

As an example, in a jeans department, there is a need to clarify the grouping between:

- *Basics*
- *Price-reduced basics and designer*
- *Full-priced single label group with manufacturer identification*
- *Skirts and shorts*
- *Jackets and coats*
- *Coveralls*
- *Tops*
- *Accessories (optional)*

Internal aisles that are 4 - 5 feet wide can make those groups clearer and more logical. *Sub-dividing merchandise into smaller visual statements is an aid that gives a shopper more time in their product search.* As long as the fixture group is no more than three fixtures deep, you can compact the fixtures, and leave single passage space between the garments.

Some merchandise categories in women's, men's, and children's departments require special fixtures. The information gathering and the merchandise planning of all departments that has been done before lays the groundwork for those decisions. Budget, availability of fixtures, materials, and scheduling comprise the elements that designers use to create the required image .

INTIMATE APPAREL

The specific needs of the intimate apparel or lingerie area are so unique that special fixtures have been in manufacturer's standard catalogs for decades. The size range of the merchandise extends from string bikinis to quilted long robes. Consideration must be given to packaged merchandise, basics and fashion, designer or manufacturer recognition for added credibility, and constant off-price sales.

Panties. The product that constantly sells more units than any other is panties. The second best selling by unit count are bras. If panties outsell bras by three to four to one, then it makes sense to give them a space and position that justifies this sales ratio. Where should they be placed in the department?

During the last several years, underpants have become that wonderfully joyous item for the retailer—the basic that became a fashion item. Panties deserve the best wall position.

The following is an example of the use of the product priority chart to select floor position and fixturing for a product.

The first priority in the selection of women's panties is the *fabric*. There are specific geographic and cultural preferences between man-made and natural fibers. For many years the proportion of 80/20 between the U.S. and Europe was reversed. American women preferred man-made fibers, while their European counterparts preferred the opposite. Today the differences on both continents has closed.

The second priority is the *hip width;* the third is *color.* After blocking the assortment by fiber, the arrangement should place colors vertically and styles horiontally.

Because of the variety of hip widths and subsequent garment lengths, I would provide maximum wall height positioning. There is nothing more wasteful or visually unfocused as creating a checkerboard pattern between the negative wall space and the equal-sized garments. This can be corrected with more visual impact when the negative space is closed. Also, add up the number of face-outs and count how many more garments can be hung making a more complete presentation in the same space using more merchandise.

With merchandise that does not drape well on a hanger, such as large size briefs, it is acceptable to shoulder hang, or side-hang. These go on rods underneath the upper face-outs, maintaining the color line if possible.

When there is a choice between items in the department of very different sizes, small items show better

on the wall and will open up more floor space for showing larger items. For example, if there were 40 robes hanging faced-out on the wall they could fill eight linear feet. The same space holding bras or panties could hold up to 700 items and still be shopped. Therefore, a secondary focal point on the wall is better used for showing bras and panties as a basic/fashion.

Bras. The issues of product priority that spurs customers to purchase are: *manufacturers brand label, fabric or material, construction, color, size, style, and price.* The layout on the wall adaptors should provide for the maximum space variation possible, both vertically and horizontally.

The essence of product presentation is the same from item to item. It starts with the sorting of priorities. and is repeated over and over again through each category.

Packaged bras and undergarments, from frilly fashion to structured support items, also come in packages. These packages, of necessity, come in a variety of sizes. Often, the manufacturer will provide a cus-

M Store, Montreal. This later version shows the growth øf the department as a result of the initial sales increase.

tom-made fixture to house their packages or open merchandise. Most are very acceptable, but store image must always be considered over manufacturer's identification.

Daywear. These items are worn under tops and bottoms. The key color to the group has the potential to sell out before back-up deliveries can be made, or unfortunately, and more commonly, will only have enough items to occupy one four-arm unit. Eighty percent or more of each daywear collection will be made from white, beige, or black. These issues must be made clear in the presentation, using height adaptors where needed for showing coordinate daywear groups.

Sleepwear and Loungewear. These items are both long and bulky or small and frilly. They can present many presentation problems that can be solved by talking to the buyers. The following questions are valid for these items and virtually all merchandise categories.

During the information gathering process, ask the buyers: "What do you believe will be your best selling item this season, and why did you buy it?" And to the area manager: "How do your customers shop?" The answers provide the merchandising needs and are the basis for a sharing of the buy/sell responsibility.

CHILDREN

The Chesick brothers ran one of the largest and most successful children's chains in North America, Au Coin des Petits, from Montreal. They believed that the item that differentiates them from other children's stores is the breadth of their outerwear merchandise in all age groups. Their reputation has kept this merchandise uppermost in the minds of their customers. They constantly reinforce it with a pre-focused arrangement.

The small sizes of children's hanging merchandise permit two-level presentations on floor fixtures. The bottom rung of a double-hung arrangement can be 30" off the floor, and the top bar is comfortable at about 54" high. On the wall, another bar can be added. Do not face-out children's clothing higher than arms-reach, because the size of the garment loses in scale to the height of the wall.

Although the lengths in clothing size vary enormously in this department, the variety of presentations needed for packages, including soft bulk items such as comforters, right into baby furniture, playpens, carriages, strollers, tricycles, and toy cars, create the need for the intelligent use of all cubic space.

Presentations of children's fashion clothing have a similarity from cul-

ture to culture. Price points create the widest differences in presentations of basics to fashion. In children's departments in many countries, the single most-bought item for children of all ages and both sexes is the disposable diaper. This item is carried in stores of all types, including supermarkets and drugstores. Should the merchandising plan for children's include diapers, then it must be placed in the department first. If not, the bulk of the items needed for on-floor stock would guarantee a major problem of placement. If the store does not carry diapers, another article that can focus the primary market position of the area must be selected from the assortment.

As in merchandising for the lingerie department, there is a need for different scale fixtures.

Wall bracket holders in the children's area should vary in on-center spacing specifically to the size of the hanger needed for each age group. A single width of 18" would accommodate most children's hanging garments. This would allow some flexibility in the use of the area, but most stores rarely move one age group to a different area.

Some type of modular platform system, such as a scaffold system for center floor elevation, is an effective means of displaying children's items.

Children have quite specific ideas of what they like to wear. The depart-

ment must relate to both the adult and the child. It is merchandise first and always on which the ambience of successful areas depend for image.

MEN'S WEAR

In men's shops that show dress wear, the product that best establishes market credibility is *ties*. In casual wear shops the product could be a variety of *tops*.

Some stores would rather rely on their assortment of dress shirts, or pants. Their importance is in their relation of the tie or top as the fashion item to the dress shirt and pants as basics. The only exceptions are stores that only carry one product. For general men's areas, a respect for the position and the adjacency of the two items is the first concern of the store designer.

Tie presentations are a signal to customers about the kind of service they will receive. If the majority of ties are hung from a hook, then the sales ethic for the area leans toward self-service. If ties are on a table, or laid flat in and on a counter case, sales-service can be expected. Tie presentations can also be made in combination with the dress shirts.

10.9

Au Coin des Petits, Montreal. The double hang of a single end-use item is perfectly acceptable, when that item is considered a single piece outfit. Each vertical section has a rationale for presentation to show different end-use products and flows from display to display.

Macy's. The use of all straight bars on a floor fixture was an early indication of how Macy's changed its merchandise policy. Bulk and clarity need not be at odds.

(10.10)

**Harry Rosen, Toronto. The
store designer made a space to show
the ties under the shirts so that the
customer would not have to turn to
coordinate the main purchase. Note
that the shirts are kept in each bin by
size, rather than by vertical color
placement.**

**Debenhams, England. The
combination of display pieces and
standard fixtures can be used to
give the sense that the merchandise
is all new.**

Dress shirt presentation can also tell
the customer what type of sales assistance is given. When shirts are in a
cube unit on the wall or the floor, the
merchandising team has two options
in the placement of the stock in the
bins.

- *Shirts can be vertically stacked
  by color within a style group
  block, with the neck sizes going
  from large on top to small on the
  bottom.* This is a reversal of the
  thinking that everything must go
  from light to dark, left to right,
  and top to bottom, small to large.
  Because size 16-1/2 necks sell
  more than 14-1/2 in most areas of
  the world that cater to
  Occidentals, it is easier to shop
  for something that is at eye
  height.
- *Different style dress or casual
  folded shirts of the same neck
  and sleeve size go into one bin.*
  This method requires sales assistance and sells more shirts more
  quickly as a salesperson shows
  the range. The proper balance
  between operating costs, profits,
  and company policy will determine the choice of presentation.
  and the correct binning.

Men's accessories are also placed
near the core of the department
called furnishings. Check the chart
that shows products by choice priority to see that the primary determi-
nant in selection making will best be
served by the equipment.

For men's clothing, suits, and
sportswear, different systems of presentation are required. The choices
between sizing first or style first has
to do with the age and fashion of the
item. Men's suits, as an example,
require that the majority of the selection be shoulder hung by size. Face-
out presentation on the wall generally
signifies the style intent of the area,
while face-hang on a floor fixture
means a full size range is available on
that fixture, and that the merchandise
is current.

The fixtures used to house men's
clothing are somewhat similar to the
needs of the women's department. I
discourage the use of single "T"
stands for the same reasons mentioned for women's clothing. Four-
arm units become the basis for the
fashion floor. But, where the round
rack is recommended for women, I
choose a straight-arm floor rack for
men. This has more to do with space
saving than it does with culture. The
bulk of the pants or jackets in the
mens area would make most merchandised round racks look like a
blob. Straight racks show the same
assortment and take up less room.
Straight racks may also be ganged
together to make a longer run needed
to justify the size range.

Chapter Eleven

Shelf Merchandise

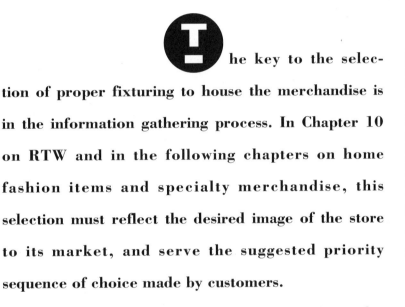he key to the selection of proper fixturing to house the merchandise is in the information gathering process. In Chapter 10 on RTW and in the following chapters on home fashion items and specialty merchandise, this selection must reflect the desired image of the store to its market, and serve the suggested priority sequence of choice made by customers.

Ready-to-wear items are generally hung for retail presentation. Virtually all other merchandise fits into three presentation classifications:

- Shelved and open for self-selection

- Packaged for hooks and stacking

- In cases for sales-service

11.1

Macy's, New York City. The Cellar evolved as a continuing fashion statement for the home. The combination of extraordinary traffic, prime location, keen product awareness, and guts in putting the assortment together, showed the way to chic presentation in a bulk format.

Virtually all home-related merchandise is shelved for presentation, from bottles to cookware cartons. Many soft items such as toys and domestics are plastic-bagged, or blister-packed, and are made to be hung from hooks. Domestics may be folded or packaged. Counters, or case-line, and special fixtures used for accessories, jewelry, cosmetics and fragrances, will be discussed in the next chapter.

Home fashion items such as domestics, housewares, china, glass, gifts, flatware, electronics, bath and closet, electrical appliances, etc., are sold primarily from shelves, most often in the manufacturer's mass-advertised and promoted packages. Designers must understand the psychology of packaging, and the specifics of the package itself in order to provide the setting and the detailed fixturing that home products require.

The Cellar in Macy's New York City store is a wonderful example of the use of manufacturer identification to give fashion credibility to housewares. When Macy's decided to change its image from the "Old Lady on 34th Street," the floor that was

remodeled first in 1976 was the lower level budget area. It became the now-famous and replicated Cellar.

Cellar merchandise is home-related, plus a food section and a drug store. Macy's relies on branded merchandise to communicate the idea of product credibility and fashion through the use of established labels. Macy's built on the success of the Cellar to move into an upgraded presentation on other floors in furniture, domestics, china and glass and lastly wearables.

Design of space for home goods must take into account the scale of the merchandise. Home merchandise items show better when the ceiling height more closely approximates the height of a room. A minimum height of 10 feet is recommended for showing items within a homelike, spatial perception. For patio furniture, the sky is literally the limit.

This chapter will outline a method that will assist designers and merchants in creating areas for home merchandise. The merchant will have determined which brands to edit from the assortment to fit into the space, and how much space is needed in order to be dominant in that category.

The product desirability chart points out customer priority choices to be respected when choosing fixtures and adaptors for home merchandise.

DOMESTICS

There is great design flexibility in a large home area for the presentation of towels. Towels are sold as open stock, with sets being organized for customers' needs from the items displayed. Towels can be folded with enough variation in width to give design latitude to the shelving. Like RTW, the wall is the starting point for planning.

Customers enter the area via an aisle from the primary entry on the floor. They then sight a place in the department that is the feature presentation leading to the first focal point. That point is at 45 degrees from the starting position, and is almost always on a wall or column. That position must contain the visual elements of a category that relates to the customers perception of product credibility.

The first priority for most buyers of towels is the manufacturer's name and style designation. It is important to show the logo of each manufacturer, kept within a size and/or color format that makes the presentation represent the image of the store, and not look like a manufacturer brand storehouse.

The width that is acceptable for most towel wall vertical lines is 12 inches. Vertical dividers can be placed to accommodate the number of colors in each manufacturer's assort-

ment. Usually, the widest assortment in color is also the selection of the retailer to represent their own chosen image. The effect of a well-composed towel wall is like a painting in fabric.

It is easiest for the staff to make a color wall by dividing the towels into three categories: cool, warm, and neutral. Any mixing of the three will generally cause problems in both tone and in visual weight. This system is called *color ribboning, color striping, or vertical colorization.* It is not advisable to place black and white at the end of the color spectrum, as they tend to drop off the palette.

Color blocking is another method that gives variation to the presentation and can assist customers in styling a bathroom. Instead of putting only one color in one stripe, it is also desirable to use two vertical color bands, and to put an analogous color or a matching print underneath the two. We see the two bands more distinctly, and the merchant also has an opportunity to display coordinates for a mix-and-match. If this is a merchandising objective, then designers must provide a space that is twice as wide as a presentation that holds one color per vertical band.

The difficulty in presenting towels is showing large and bulky items such as bath sheets in the same line as washcloths. Different depths and widths are needed. Since all merchants want to show a rolled edge

11.2

Printemps, Paris. When manufacturers promote brand awareness, smart stores delineate their towel stock by using their names and logos. In the current overseas market, the most widely creditable U.S. products are its towels.

Fieldcrest. The smallest towels are placed at eye level, within arm's reach.

Globus, Switzerland. A lead-off column is built out to four feet to hold an assortment of disposable basics that are sold in the bath shop. A key to the quality of the merchandise is forecast by the selection of basics on the column.

forward, even the wash cloths are doubled which further reduces their depth. There is a merchandising rule of thumb that the smaller the towel, the greater the margin for profit. Smaller units are then placed in the horizontal center of the wall with the larger towels on top or bottom. Some presentations have reserved space for seat covers, mats, and rugs dyed to the same colors, plus soap and ceramic decorative items.

Towel sizes range from bath sheet, bath towel, face towel, fingertip, to washcloth. The amount of vertical space given to each particular item is in proportion to the way that customers buy the unit quantities. Be sure to ask the merchant, "How do your customers buy a group of towels?" Make no assumptions, because there are radical changes from culture to culture.

For example, bath sheets are not common in Oriental cultures. In a Singapore store, I saw a presentation that seemed totally disassorted. Major space was devoted to wash cloths and relatively minor space to face towels, with no bath sheets showing. The reason was the proportion in which customers bought this item. They purchased 12 wash cloths to every face towel, because they used the wash cloths to wipe their hands and face between the courses of each meal.

Bath shops stock a wide variety of items at different price points. Since *the bathroom is the room most frequently changed in a home*, it makes good merchandising sense to accommodate an assortment that can be the style-setter for the domestics area.

BEDDING

Customers look for color first when selecting sheets and pillowcases. Pattern and price must also be acceptable before most customers consider the manufacturer or the designer. This merchandise group is displayed by manufacturer first, mainly because a mix of the graphics from all resources printed on the overwrap would cheapen the look.

A recent trend to standardize the packaging for sheets and pillow cases has helped designers select modular floor and wall units to house the packages. In most instances, the display fixture of choice is a glass cube unit. The best units are made with the shelves slightly tilted back so that when a few items are bought, the remainder do not fall forward. Vertical space should be permitted for customers to reach the last package without scraping their knuckles.

Although the uniform sizing of the packaging of sheets has helped to standardize the container, the variety of sheet sizes within a particular style

is a presentation problem. The full range of sheets includes queen, king, double, and twin. Each of those sizes has both flat sheets and fitted bottom sheets. Some stores also carry a full line of long sheets. Pillow cases in the United States are generally two rectangular sizes, but in many other cultures square and bolster shapes are available. This means that for each style there may be 10 to 12 cubes needed just to hold a packaged group.

Packaged pillows, blankets, and comforters comprise some of the most difficult items to house. They are the least productive in terms of space taken to sales volume and are the bulkiest items in the bedding category. Constant maintenance of the floor display is critical.

The choices of wall or center floor positions present a dilemma for both the retailer and the designer. However, if we follow the same concept mentioned in the RTW section, that small items fit best on the wall in terms of the amount of space taken for the number of SKUs, then the smaller sheet and pillowcase packages go onto the wall, and the more bulky items are placed into floor bins, shelves, or cubes.

In order to give ambient display to the assortment properly, consider the amount of floor space that it takes to use a bed of any size. Even though it is most natural to see a regular bed

on the floor rather than a truncated version, the amount of available floor space will determine how and if floor displays will be used.

An interesting variant is accomplished by making a display with a mattress-type pallet on the wall or above the valance line. For this, designers can provide plugs that can be taken down, dressed, returned, and lit to change the bedding patterns either seasonally or as new patterns arrive.

The nuances of design can take a dowdy bed and bath area and make it charming and responsive to the needs of the store and its customers.

11.3

Top left : Nouvelle Galeries, France. In European stores, the large number of sizes and variety of styles of sheets and pillowcases change the packaging sufficiently to warrant an adjustable shelf placement.

Top right: Specialty store. The tightness of space in this specialty store makes vertical displays a necessity.

Bottom left: Debenhams, England. A bedding boutique within a larger department that carries a designer 's or a manufacturer's complete line is called a shop-in-shop.

Bottom right: Debenhams, England. Center floor positions for any merchandise require screens or stacks of merchandise that will stop the eye before it reaches the distant wall.

WINDOW TREATMENT

Curtains, drapes, and blinds can be shown with back lighting and front lighting. When placed against a wall, the items shown become a vignette, and appear the way that customers normally see these items.

Customers make their selection of window treatment first by the style, then color, and then price. Category groupings must respect this order. Even though the purchase of ready-made packaged items is the way that customers take the items from the store, the decision to buy a particular item is made after viewing and probably touching the material.

J.C. Penney has a gained a major share of this market (approximately 35 percent). Visit a Penney's store and note the space store design devoted to product display. Adopting techniques to fit different spaces and assortments can lead to nuances that better serve a retailer's needs, and may in turn be equally innovative.

CHINA, GLASS, AND GIFTS

China: All items in this category are functional; many also have an intrinsic value. There are casual, designer, and fine categories. The store designer must develop a method to show all of the categories, side by side, in the same or contiguous areas. *Their methods for presentation are essentially determined by the amount of merchandise needed to represent a combination of clarity and credibility.*

With fine china (also referred to as porcelain or bone) it is important to have space to show at least the dinner plate, cup, and saucer. Some of the key sets should present the remainder of the set as well as all the serving pieces. There are approximately 1,000 fine china designs from which to choose. The selection of this item is the key to the bridal business. When the bridal area is marketed well by the retailer, it can have about 40 to 60 percent of the entire business in china and glass.

Customers select their china pattern, either fine or casual, from the style of the dinner plate. Some stores have a "shooting gallery" effect by simply lining up the total assortment of dinner plates horizontally on shelves. At one time, the major division was a separation of bone and porcelain. (Bone china, literally using the ground shin bone of an ox, is creamier in tone than porcelain, which by comparison is cool white.) Now, the differences in the clay composition are less important, and the staff can choose any number of styles from the shape of the profile to the design of the pattern to start their presentation ethic.

(11.4)

(facing page) Croscill Inc. showroom, New York City. Many manufacturers put together some of the best presentations of their merchandise, whether in their showrooms or at a trade show. Buyers, who go to the market and see these presentations, should be encouraged and permitted to assist in the selection of the method of their store's presentation.

(11.5)

(above) Cemaco, Guatemala. This glass-cube column was constructed around a support column. It holds an enormous amount of sample stock and is merchandised vertically to ease selection.

(11.6)

Printemps, France. The architectural detail of the lit arch is the visual theme that unites the individual manufacturer presentations. In the departments, the names of the brands are kept within the arch.

Presentation made by dinner plates alone does not give the customer a focus, especially of those patterns that have been consistent best sellers. Without knowledgeable sales assistance, customers can be quickly swamped by the overabundance of patterns for selection.

It has become fashionable and practical to compose the selection by manufacturer grouping first. The customer looks for, and is shown, similar styles within each manufacturer group. As mentioned in the towel section, control of signing and design of the component manufacturer boutiques creates a space that represents the store image, rather than a manufacturer showroom.

Two methods can be utilized by the designer that employ two of the aesthetic principles discussed earlier: *vertical image and interrupted pattern.* For example, in the midst of a line of dinner plates, designers can place a niche that would hold the service pieces of the best-selling pattern. This can be repeated a few times as wall space permits. With adjustable shelving, the china pieces

can be placed from top to bottom in order of service. It is a technique that helps customers understand how the merchandise relates to their needs.

When center floor positions are taken for china, units can be built that show the dinner plates vertically. Column-surround units or dummy columns can be incorporated into the design scheme. A four-sided glass cube unit with light at the top and a mirror at the back virtually makes the column disappear. It offers numerous opportunities for shifting the merchandise to present ideas for set purchasing, individual items for gift giving, or coffee and dessert sets. The best-selling pattern or the pattern that the retailer wishes to promote is placed at eye level, flanked vertically by other patterns in order of their desirability. Other items in the style are placed horizontally, in order of use.

Casual china: There are many variations of manufacture and pricing within this category. In the shopper's mind, a major difference between casual and fine china is the amount of time needed to purchase and get it home. The ability to take home a package of casual china, rather than ordering and waiting for a delivery of fine china, is a factor for selection and multiple stocking needs.

Several of the best selling patterns must be kept in full range and depth,

(11.7)

referred to as "open stock." This means that the pattern will be available until the manufacturer decides not to produce it any longer. When the manufacturer discontinues the style, the store notifies the pattern's previous purchasers, and encourages replacement, or addition to the set, prior to closing out.

Provision must be made for housing an amount of open stock that contains the components for a service for four place settings, multiplied by timely anticipated customer demand. Proper merchandising presentation has a dual edge. It clearly tells shoppers what their choices are, and also provides a unique source of inventory control for the retailer. Visual sighting is the fastest way that the staff has of noting actual or forthcoming shortages of stock. Presentations that respect customer priority in choice give added value in control.

Glassware and Stemware: Improved manufacturing in methods have blurred the idea of crystal (leaded glass) from housewares or non-leaded glass. Houseware glass can be shown in open stock or in sets, while crystal is generally shown in sets with one sample per item. There are several manufacturers who now produce leaded glass in quantities, and distribute them in well-designed packages. Bulk presentation is made now more by price point than by glass content.

Shelf space is provided for all glass with many floor cubes or bunkers used for display of packages. What color is best used for backing to show the clear glass? Most designers opt for a cool color backing, believing that an icy look augments the effect. Since color preference is personal, I might suggest that warm colors be considered.

One of the major mistakes in lighting glass comes from the assumption that glass is better when it is bottom-lit. The best use for bottom lighting is when the glass is frosted. But, since this is a very minor proportion of drinking glass, the best presentations that I have seen is when each shelf is lit from the position above, and the shelf surface is the same color and material as the backing. I recommend this so that customers do not look into the source of light, but rather see the glass itself as the highest intensity. Eyes move to the light, and if the source of the illumination is prime, then the iris diaphragm closes down, and it is more difficult to see the subject.

Depth of stock is a determining factor in presenting houseware glass. Since most purchases of non-leaded glass are not made in sets, for different purposes, but by single item, in multiples, the choice for retailers and customers is narrowed. There are several sizes in tumblers, but not as much variety as found in stemware.

Printemps, France. Open stock that may be purchased by the piece or by the set. The top shelf is for display of the line and the two bottom shelves are for stock.

Rheinbrucker, Switzerland. This sister store to Printemps shows the assortment on the shelves and the display above using a tilted mirror to duplicate the setting in a unique, intelligent manner. Customers relate to a setting for two rather than a single place setting.

Eaton's, Toronto. This delightful rendition of a wall shelf rhythm combined with excellent lighting and warm color represents a collaboration between sensitive designers and knowledgeable merchants.

(11.8)

Bloomingdales, New York. The Main Course, a floor devoted to home fashion, contains many types of gift departments that can be adjusted to take on a promotional stance as the store decides its assortment theming.

The provision for quantity follows a formula that corresponds to the past sales history, plus anticipated future sales. On-floor, in-stock positions should not make the area look like a warehouse, but should always keep the individual items in enough depth to appear creditable.

For instance, if the average purchase for tumblers by one customer equals eight items, and the history shows that the item sells to four customers per week, then the on-hand position must hold 32 glasses, plus an additional 32 to meet the criteria of in-stock credibility and potential additional sales. If normal deliveries are made once every two weeks then an additional 32 should be on hand or in reserve. Without a stockroom, the floor must hold the full complement. Designers cannot account for operational efficiency or deficiency, but they can assist retailers to appreciate the effect that the quantity of stock can have on sales made in anticipation of a good seller, and try

to prevent out-of-stock situations.

Since appearance of depth is important in basic housewares and unpackaged glass, it may prove useful to increase the illusion of more stock by putting a mirror at the back of shelving units. Mirror backs with boxes or opaque merchandise is ineffective and costly.

Gifts: Home fashion gift items, the more volatile and seasonally sensitive merchandise of this department, are usually displayed for convenient customer inspection. The typical division of products is by material, rather than by function. Ceramics, glass, metallics, wood, fiber, marble, candles, etc. are subdivisions of the gift grouping. When properly merchandised throughout the year, they may be regrouped to be put together by color, room of use, surface finish, theme, or subject.

Not only should the fixtures be adaptable for changing merchandise, but the areas must also have the potential for making different statements. For example, Christmas as the most important time for gift-giving needs potential for holding higher stock levels without appearing to be in mass stock. Customers have specific ideas of items they wish to acquire for themselves, or to give as gifts for someone else. A table setting may be ornamented with candles, flowers, napkin holders, and favors. Red is the Christmas color, so items should be put together with red in mind as the principal binder. Price point groupings attract customers with a large shopping list.

During the rest of the year, the gift department can reflect the theme of the month. Mother's Day increases the sales of vanity table items from fragrance bottles to picture frames. Father's Day shows a higher demand in the desk top category. Thanksgiving items dress the dining table. The flexibility of this department makes it an ideal place to lead customers into the table top areas.

PEG-HOOKED OR HANGING PACKAGES

A wide variety of merchandise is offered for sale in plastic film sacks and shrink-wrapped blister packages. Merchandise as diverse as fry pans, health and beauty aids, hardware, costume jewelry, food, and kitchen gadgets are not over-wrapped and are also hung from hooks.

Fixturing decisions for packaged merchandise of this type are determined by the vertical dimension of the package. Selecting slatwall or pegboard for the backing is a matter of both economics and aesthetics. Whichever is chosen, the important issue is the vertical spacing that permits one item to hang above another and allows enough space for clear-

ance without creating a checkerboard pattern of background and item. As an example, small packages that measure 3 inches vertically can be put on hooks from a slatwall that is grooved at 3-inch intervals. In order to avoid overlap, the presentation will have equal spacing between the positive and the negative space that gives a pattern to the whole without first creating a focus.

When making subdivisions of merchandise in a larger category of items that come packaged for hanging, first look at the type face, color, and graphics. The width of the space needed is first determined by the design of the package, and then by the material finish of the merchandise. It is absolutely essential to keep vertical lines of merchandise, as this method of packaging may be one of the hardest for customers to find their needs.

PACKAGED OR BOXED ITEMS

Manufacturers have found an important sales aid when purchasers leave the store with their products in aesthetically pleasing carry-home boxes. Some packages become their own signs when displayed in multiples on shelves or on pallets, and have been printed with different images on the four sides of the box. Sections of the same photo are printed on each side.

11.9

Macy's, New York. This is the way that the manufacturer holds shelf space with intelligence in packaging.

Dillards, Little Rock. Even when the picture is the same, the use of solid blocks of red and green extend the presence of the item giving it more visual importance as an idea for a Christmas gift.

11.10

Former Korvettes store, New York. The image clearly communicated is that the store presents small electrics well. Unfortunately, the selection was wide, rather than narrow and deep.

Ann and Hope, Rhode Island. Two display shelves permit irons to be coordinated with steamers. Toasters should then be teamed with microwaves and sandwich grilles.

When the four faces are placed side by side, they create a picture that has four times the impact.

For designers, the merchandising of boxed items has just as much to do with aesthetics and practicality as the finest piece of RTW. As mentioned in Chapter 9, the height of the stack must be maintained so that the item for handling or viewing is at eye level. The stack of boxes from a pallet or on shelving should contain enough units to go from bottom to top. When the boxes are oversize, more than one stack can be on floor pallets or the balance held in reserve. When the boxes are small, it is necessary to have a two-strip face-out presentation in order to give the item some vertical presence.

At least one item should be open for inspection, placed on top of the stack or on a shelf. If it is not open, then you may be assured that it will be by customers. Testing of electric-powered items should be confined to a specified area convenient for both the shopper and the staff.

Chapter Twelve

Cosmetics, Jewelry, and Accessories

What are the most difficult items to merchandise? The general consensus of retailers and designers is that the smaller the item, the more the finesse required. Jewelry, cosmetics, fragrances, and accessories are items that present the greatest challenges, yet offer the most opportunity to set the style for the attitude customers develop toward the store. This is not because of the housing, or the servicing, but because of the variety of options that the retailer exercises toward their service, sense of exclusivity, and their location.

They are generally treated like high fashion items, because many carry a high price tag. However, if we closely examine each category, the same rules that apply to other merchandise concerning basics or fashion hold true for these small items. The major difference is that they generate an extraordinary high volume of sales per square foot. As an issue, sales per square foot is deceiving. A more accurate measure of a product's contribution to the general health of the company is the profit per square foot that it generates. Keep that in mind as we examine the products and the fixturing and service that they require.

In all product categories of accessories, jewelry or cosmetics, the major part of the assortment is basic. That is, 80 percent of each group is standard, and only 20 percent is volatile, or fashion. It is the latter group that is heavily promoted and heavily marked-down. The in-store placement and the outside advertising make the products highly visible. In department stores, these products are in prime traffic locations.

They are given a glamour treatment in presentation. In this framework the use of the word "commodity" may sound strange. Yet, reduced to the elements of the merchandise itself, certain similarities may be noted that changes the perception of each range of product line.

COSMETICS AND FRAGRANCES

Ask some questions about the generally accepted stock balance of the fragrance category.

- *How many fragrances does a shop carry?*
- *What percentage of those have been in the assortment for more than one year?*
- *How many have never changed their packaging?*
- *How many are on a replacement system?*

The answers to these questions could fit many items in the housewares category. The major difference is the price compared to the bulk of the package. Aside from the glamorous photos of models, the amount of sales service that the items warrant, and the need for security, there is really very little difference to the essential merchandising individual items, in cosmetics or housewares.

Designers and merchants should understand that the best way to present fragrances and cosmetics is to give customers the sense that the merchandise will be in stock as long as the manufacturer is in business. Product credibility is gained by showing customers depth in the line, especially in the stocking of the best-selling unit in fragrance, the two-ounce spray cologne. It is a com-

12.1

Proffitts, Tennessee. The design of this department resembles a quasi-medical skin care clinic. The desk-top lamps also give a personal, rather than a corporate look.

modity. Just like an iron, it is sold in an unopened package with a tester unit for inspection.

The typical method of presentation of fragrances is in a counter. When provided, the product is placed in a back case. Service is essential by sales people called consultants. Shelf life is short because of the alcoholic content, so product rotation is necessary. Both the counter and the back case need lighting to further enhance the item. High-quality package and bottle design and extensive media promotion contribute to easy customer recognition. The structural housing of the units should not compete with the individual product designs, but should work to unite the effect of the whole department.

Many manufacturers who wish to maintain a strict visual identity have designed their own product presentation areas to show the corporate image consistently from store to store. The fact that identical units placed in neighboring stores are competing for the same customer in the same market is not as important to manufacturers as keeping to their design standards. These situations usually turn on the balance of the strength of the store name to the manufacturer's product line in each market.

Stores with a strong market presence have the option to supersede the manufacturer's and impose their own

visual aesthetic over each manufacturer in the entire category. The major visual impact of the manufacturer is consumer association with the packaging, the graphics, and the logo. This occurs when the counters and cases show the stock clearly and dramatically. Sales personnel are usually representatives of the manufacturer. They are well trained in product presentation as part of their work. Many times they dress in a uniform that keeps the presence of the the manufacturer apart from its competitors.

Some stores maintain a single area as a fragrance boutique that combines the presentation of all fragrances. The presentation of the collection of those packages follows the same rules as other products. The best seller is placed in the prime sighting position flanked on either side by the next best sellers. Some discretionary choice is made within the remainder of the grouping permitting an alternating pattern of dark and light. This furthers the clarity of each line within a vertical composition. This is generally accomplished on a back wall or case. The change of size varies as much as the range of box sizes in housewares. For this reason, variable shelf height is recommended. The counter in front of the case may hold samples of the lines, or be used for promotional purposes.

Cosmetics that range from skin toners to skin treatments are also part of the assortment. Most manufacturers have a strict manual for placement. Many of these guides follow a similar logic. Since lipstick is the best-selling item in the entire

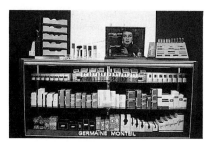

(12.2)

Germaine Monteil. This sample case shows how to place items in a limited space when the entire line is presented. From colors to lotions and cleansers to fragrances, each shelf has a rhythm and uses the package size and color to make each line clearer.

Merle Norman. A top shelf for color may be used in a display format to show a wide variety of impulse items.

range of products in an entire general merchandise store, it is preferable to give the top shelf to the lipsticks surrounded by blushes and eye shadows. These products give the display the greatest range of color which is preselected by the manufacturer to go with seasonal and current fashion demands.

A second or third shelf may hold lotions or other skin care products. Because these packages are small they may have to be double-faced or double-tiered. This is done to prevent the space above or along side of the package to be greater than the con-

tainer. Once again, it is the negative space issue. The bulk of all the assembled items should be visually more important than the empty space.

When planning a center-floor cosmetics area, it is preferable to place the back case in line with, and incorporate the columns. This removes the obstruction of the column from the open space and/or counter area needed for direct contact between the sales person and the client.

JEWELRY

Three main sub-divisions exist in jewelry—fine, bridge, and costume. As implied in the names, the type of service will extend from full sales assistance to self-selection.

Fine jewelry is the most standard and classical of the three, and consists of most of the collection's basic items. Because of its price points, customers expect to see these items in the cases, and to have a sales person nearby. They are also items that are placed behind the counter in trays or folios that are brought out as customers define what they are looking for. For most customers the sequence of selection for an item of fine jewelry starts with the purpose then price, and then style within the material finish.

The design of the counter should accommodate a glass vitrine that is

14 to 16 inches high. The height of the counter (38 to 47 inches) and the front design are made for the comfort of either a standing or seated patron. Tilted pads in the vitrine make it easier to see the assortment and to have more square area on which to place the jewelry.

Jewelry counter design sometimes defeats the purpose of showing the assortment clearly. Designers and display personnel place obstacles in the case that divert the customer's attention from items for sale. For example, imagine a vitrine that has a mirror back and sides. It reflects the back of the holder or item, and bits of things that the staff wishes concealed. Many times it is not a mirror that causes the problem, but different surfaces and different colors.

Why not simplify the presentation devices? Why not provide a case backing that is the same color as the pads? Why not take advantage of current technology and use a curved glass front which virtually eliminates reflection?

Overhead pin spots in a line over the cases will light the items, form a light valance, and add to the sparkle. Each light becomes another point source that creates another angle of reflected brilliance.

The initial design may include small covered platforms that assist in separating categories within a major group. If a second shelf is needed,

then do not use glass. Without pads, customers see through from the top shelf down, creating a confusion of images. When the bulk of the assortment calls for more than one shelf, use a step-back, tilt system.

All shelves should be fabric-covered, and have a built-in tube light to illuminate the items on the lower shelves. The shelf's surface should allow for pinning.

Bridge jewelry items fall between fine and costume jewelry in price and in purpose. Their appeal may lie in the intrinsic worth of the materials (fine metals and semi-precious stones) and/or the design. The term "bridge jewelry" was created by department store buyers who wished to have a category of merchandise to fill a price point need. The primary items that were first developed and are still the heart of the assortment are 14K chains and earrings.

12.3

An interesting design gone awry. The glass shelves and sparse placement of stock confuse and distract rather than focus.

These metal pierced panels were designed to hold a wide variety of prepackaged, inexpensive costume jewelry. Note the depth of stock on each hook.

(12.4)

Foot Locker. Brand name is the first priority in the mind of the customer for athletic shoes.

Nordstrom, Seattle. Women's shoes are shown by style first and then by color. Left and right are shown at all times.

The cost of bridge jewelry may run as high as some of the fine jewelry. Each store may put a different definition on the boundaries of bridge jewelry. Once the buyer tells the store designer the reasons why the items were bought, their placement becomes virtually automatic. Price alone puts all jewelry of this category in cases. Display should show the real "bridge" quality of the visual transition from fine to costume.

Bridge jewelry's success led to designer jewelry. When Tiffany's wanted to have a price point below fine jewelry, they cultivated and promoted Elsa Perretti and Paloma Picasso. Their innovative designs created a new value to basic material. Another tier of design consideration was made by introducing art jewelry that required a new presentation mode.

Costume jewelry provides the seasonal flavor. These items may be considered as a clothing accessory, and can either be in cases or open for selection. They are shown in multiples on self-service units. Case pads for backing should permit color changes for the season or the promotion. A second set of pads is a great option. They can be recovered and can cut the time of the change to keep the case fresh and current. The sales rate of costume jewelry necessitates the presentation of more than one item, or card, per hook.

SHOES

Accessories are the finishing touches on a RTW ensemble, and belong in the basic/fashion category. Shoes, a replaceable basic/fashion accessory, are primarily staff serviced, and can be the reason for shoppers to choose one store over another as their favorite. The width of the selection in one store should fulfill the need to comparative shop further.

Women are less brand loyal than men. About 60 percent of male shoppers will chose brand first, while about 35 percent of women shoppers think of brand first. Men prefer to shop in specialty stores, while women will choose a department store or a store that carries many brands.

Except for sale periods when the primary selection factor is size, as it is for all clothing categories, the choice of the shoe generally starts with style for purpose, then color. For security reasons, many stores still insist on displaying only the left shoe of the pair. However, the most successful shoe departments in the world, in the Nordstrom chain, show their shoes in pairs open for selection. Their women's shoes are assembled first by style. Men's shoes are assembled by manufacturer. In each grouping there is a very wide assortment at a variable price range.

ATHLETIC SHOES

Sales of athletic shoes have grown to become a major part of any shoe collection. Their market share growth has resulted in specialty stores and departments that service only this product. These stores often have an athletically technical oriented sales staff. In presentation, the priorities of these stores range from manufacturer's choice to usage, style, and price. Fixture producers have a range of devices that hold shoes. Most hold only one or two shoes. This does not account for showing a grouping of five or six different colors within a style, or five styles within a color. Designers need to specify the variety of types necessary to meet the intent of the store in presentation for walls, floor, and window.

Customers choose this product based on manufacturer, use, size range, style, and price. Manufacturer loyalty stems from the belief in consistent fit, and serviceability.

HANDBAGS

As important as handbags are to the sales of the category of accessories, they have been given one of the worst fixtures ever invented for merchandise presentation. On walls and on floor units designers select—and

stores use—the underslung waterfall "J" hook. The original concept was customer convenience. Customers could pick off a bag from one arm without having to take off the bags in front. However, when bags are open for self-selection, more than one bag of the same color and style is bought, and put on one arm. The net effect is a visually dismal repetition of straps in a sharp triangular pattern which makes the face of the bag, the real seller, less important. With this fixture, on a wall or floor unit, the straps account for more than half of the ver-

tical space. They take away from the impact of the group. Waterfall "J" hooks should *never* be used!

The best way to show bags is on shelves. On the wall, floor, or in cases, a bag is sold by seeing the face. When there are multiples in the assortment, the placement of the back-up items can be the gusset, or side, out. Shelf depth should vary from top to bottom to allow for overhead lighting to hit each shelf. Additional service is required, but the question to ask is, "Do you wish to sell them, or stock them?"

12.5

Strap-hanging handbags. This display forces attention on the strap rather than on the face design of the handbag on which the customer will make the buying decision.

Bermans, Minneapolis. The amount of merchandise is greater than any that can be had by hanging. Yet, the sculpting of the wall clearly shows customers what the merchant considers to be the items it wishes to sell.

(12.6)

Hosiery is a basic/fashion item that has held its fashion position for two decades with the help of good packaging and themed displays.

Rheinbrucker, Switzerland. The amount of bulk does not decrease the fashion acceptance of the item.

HOSIERY

Hosiery, once considered as an accessory to lingerie, is a strong main-floor item. When panty hose became more important than individual pairs of hose, the wide variety of manufacturers' packages created a fixturing nightmare on the sales floor. Adding to the problems of presentation were manufacturer-supplied fixtures. Many of these fixtures were designed to hold a specific type of package. They were even used after the item was sold out and never replaced. The result was chaos, as volatile sales created half-filled and poorly maintained units.

Standardization of packaging has permitted a latitude to the store in the selection and the changing of the lines as styles and colors vary. Stationery-type holders are used, sometimes 12 tiers high, to present panty hose on a wall. The space above has been creatively turned into a fine display area that requires prop mounting and lighting. Lesser-tiered units on the floor are also needed.

SOFT ACCESSORIES

Other accessories such as scarfs, shawls, ties, socks, hair ornaments, hats, belts, umbrellas, glasses, and specialty items can be shown in a variety of ways. The type of fixtures and adapters used to show and to house accessories are primarily dependent on the balance between the price and the degree of customer service supplied by the retailer.

The golden rule of accessory presentation for the designer to live by is: *no matter what the presentation mode, or the amount of service offered, the accessories shown should never look out-of-stock or disheveled.* The appearance of accessory presentation gives customers their initial impression of the type of service and the exclusivity level of the entire store.

Signing

etail signs must be: 1: legible; and 2: uniquely attractive.

Signs are the first element of recognition and retention by customers. There are definite signals that signs send to customers. The size of the sign, its location, the color, and the type or script carry meanings that designers should be aware of before incorporating a sign into the design.

There are some inherent paradoxes to the resolution of physical aesthetic realities of signs to their intellectual interpretation. Most standards of judgment will be long-lasting, while others change with the current fashions.

OoLaLa. Designers must not use neon against a mirror background. It makes the sign illegible when lit.

Standa, Italy. A discount store sign in perfect keeping with the corporate ethic.

FACADE OR BUILDING SIGN

Signs outside a shop should be lit, either from front spots or from a backlighting system. There are signs that use a panel of light, and place letters on the glowing backpanel, much the same way that cinema marquees are illuminated. Some signs use chaser lights around the perimeter, or a sequential moving system on the letters. As we explore the different techniques, we will see how a similar pattern emerges. The more visually aggressive the sign is, the lower the perceived price point of the merchandise.

Neon letters are seen more clearly from greater distances than any other form of signing. This is because we look directly into the source of illumination. Even though there are many wonderful current art pieces and signs that use neon, the association has been with items of a commodity nature, bars and diners. This should not discourage its use, but should direct its use toward a youthful and fun appeal. Mirrors used as a backing for neon doubles the image, making it virtually illegible from any direction, except head-on.

Backlighting individual letters of a sign makes them stand from the background better than frontlit letters of the same hue and tone. Backlit signs work better at night than day. Because of the control of light in an enclosed mall, most shops use backlit letters. In more recent mall construction, and on the street, where daylight filters onto the facade, designers should be sure there is sufficient contrast of the letter to the background.

Another method of backlighting is specifying opaque letters that stand away from the wall. The illumination is from behind the letters; it lights the wall and halos the letters, and works better at night. This method gives the impression of higher exclusivity to the store.

Raised letters placed on the surface, lit or unlit from behind, give a dimensional effect during a sunny day, but tend to flatten out on an overcast day. These signs should be lit from the front so that the dimensional shadow effect will be present at night.

A sophisticated method that is receiving more attention today is the intaglio, or carved, incised letter. It creates a classic effect where the shadow is the same as raised letters.

Some stores use plaques that are applied to the building, either over the main entry, or at the side of the entry. The size of the plaque in proportion to the scale of the facade play an inverse role in customer's thinking. The larger the percentage of space taken to the size of the facade or the entry by the sign, the less the exclusivity and possibly price, without necessarily lessening the value to the customer. Merchants may request that the designer use the company logo on the store.

The choices of color combinations of letters and background must be considered for their dual effect of legibility and value perception. The most legible combination, black on a yellow ground, however, indicates to the shopper a lower price, best value, non-exclusive store. This does not mean that a sign must be illegible or monochromatic to represent mid-high to high price and exclusivity perception. There are unlimited combinations based on taste, timing, and local market biases.

Marshall Field, Chicago. Script and backlighting are combined for a mall store entrance.

Bergdorf Goodman, New York City. A large sign is not needed for this upscale store which relies on past customer identification and a high-traffic location.

Loblaws, Toronto. A food warehouse off a main thoroughfare draws customers with a stencil letter logo painted on a corrugated metal.

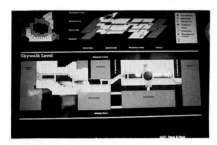

13.3

**Most customers
find that simple
architectural plans
are not too technical
to use for directional
information.**

DIRECTORIES

Most infrequent and first-time shoppers need directory signs and area category signs, to find their way. In shopping centers and malls, architects often use the shopping center floor plan to locate the individual shops. With color coding for merchandise or geographic area, most shoppers can read them. Maps must be accompanied by listing the category, followed by a listing of product, which is then alphabetized by the name of the store and colorized by general merchandise category. Newly developed computerized touch screen systems give shoppers a clear visual presentation for wayfinding.

In department or large specialty stores, customers use a directory to locate the floor that has the merchandise they are interested in. In elevators or on escalators, signs give customers additional information. Once reaching the floor, the sign can point out the various sub-divisions in the categories.

DEPARTMENTAL IDENTIFICATION

In large specialty or department stores, departmental signing also involves the operational and the merchandising sectors of the company. *Some companies prefer to use mer-*

chandise itself as the sign of the area. This works well when the merchandise is sub-divided first by end use. In a woman's area, coats, lingerie, dresses, separates, etc., are easily differentiated. Some signs can identify an area that contains merchandise that has been bought to express a season or a promotional attitude that can be given a name, and a graphic flavor that is temporary. These signs use words that signify what the merchandise represents.

Another type of sub-division of merchandise presentation that needs specific signing are designer/manufacturer boutiques or private label signature shops. Here customers are expected to have some previous idea of the styling and the pricing of the merchandise in this area. The store may put together a department with a variety of logos. If done within an aesthetic that is controlled by an overall store policy, it can create the effect of having many choices within the range of the store selection.

Departmental or area signs represent the last area of the expected responsibility of the store designer to the commitment of design consistency. However, I suggest that designers carry the unity of their conceptions into other signing, including provisions for rack signs.

PRODUCT INFORMATION, PROMOTION, PRICE

I have found less consistency in the design of these signs than in almost any other area of the store. Within a single store, they may vary in the size, placement, color, typeface, and information format. There is no possible way that a store designer can impose a consistent ethic on signs that are changed as often as the merchandise, or when the next ad hits the newspapers. *Other than designing a full manual for signing, which would last about as long as the next shift in personnel or the next 'critical' clearance, the designer and the merchant should outline a policy that would permit designers to incorporate sign holders or positions for signs. In this manner there would be a consistency for the size of the signs that are used for any informational purpose.*

The selection of the sign holder should be considered as part of the visual scheme and incorporated into sign policy that takes into account all the permanent and current needs of the company.

• *Conran's/Habitat*
Their signs fit within their company's approach to its simple, practical, aesthetically pure merchandise. The area signs are printed in black capitals on a white ground with a thin

13.4

Conran's, New York. The type set signs, stencil product signs, and script information signs work together, yet signify different purposes.

(13.5)

The Limited. The chain currently uses a more stylish sign as a banner. As large as they are, they fit the atmosphere of the store. It is also chic to use black and white in a fashion photo.

line red grid. The store sign uses upper and lower case letters. This follows through into the product signs, where the store has involved the staff and permitted hand-written signs in a selected size frame. The continuation of the grid pattern links the overhead area signs to the eye level product and price signs. The grid also serves as a guide for stenciled letters that can be created by each store's staff.

Distinctive product information signs have white letters against a black background. There may be a small drawing to accompany the cursive script writing. The text relates to special uses or interesting tidbits of information about the product. Longer duration signs are centrally printed and distributed. Signs of a more immediate nature are executed by the store staff. Handwritten signs that are kept neat, legible, and distinct, tend to be another visual bridge formed between customers and staff.

• **The Limited**
The Limited is an case study in excellence in the use of graphics, euphonious wording, and intelligence in message.

When the chain was in its early growth stage, it used cardboard prisms declaring "REAL SALE" or "REAL DEAL SALE" with a simple price at the bottom. The letters were white drop-out on a deep-tone background. Later signs announced "2 for l", "3 for 2", or "4 for $10.00", thus selling more units and eliminating the need for customers to compute fractions or percentages. The idea of using dropout letters on a dark ground works better to contain the sign in space, rather than the letters printed on a white ground. Another era of Limited signing introduced the color photo showing a model in a coordinated outfit, with garments being shown on the rack. The Limited hardly ever puts sale merchandise on the wall. Their wall merchandise presentation is used to tell the current story without words.

Victoria's Secret, the lingerie shops owned by The Limited, uses calligraphic script for its signs to add an air of personal intimacy to the message. The Limited logo signs on the outside of the building or mall shops changed with the growth and repositioning of the company.

(13.6)

**Loblaw's, Toronto: Graphics are used
here as a decorative element. In a
cubic space that is large and must
turn fresh produce at least every two
weeks, the size of the signs sets a
price point and allows the customer
to focus on the product.**

SUPERMARKETS

Possibly no store type needs the use
of signing more than supermarkets.
Yet, with a few exceptions, I find
supermarket signing inadequate and
unappealing. Some of the best signs
that I have seen are in supermarkets
outside the U.S. Loblaw's, a
Canadian chain, virtually took sign
graphics to new heights when it com-
missioned a store designer to do the
entire supermarket as one graphics
package. This bold move, in coordination with a new merchandise
policy, saved the chain.

INFORMATION AND
POSITIONING

Signs and signing techniques are just
another bridge that spans the company's intent and identity to give a
clear message to customers. Signs tell
customers not only where they are in
the store, but also where the store is
in their market position.

Lighting

If we agree that the store is theater, then the merchandise is the star. The objective of retail lighting design is to light the merchandise, glamorize it, and make it appealing to the audience, the shoppers.

Lighting creates an atmosphere that matches the desired merchandise value–the balance between exclusivity and commodity. The store is a bare stage with no scenery, the lines to be delivered are fine products. The backstage crew is the staff of the store, the merchandise represents the cast of characters, the fixtures are the props. Successful productions can be mounted with those elements, plus the addition of intelligent lighting. Lighting evokes a powerful mood and creates an atmosphere that makes the customer's experience memorable, and helps to sell more merchandise.

(14.1)

Byerly's, Minnesota. Note the different types and positions for lighting instruments. The effect of incandescents on the fresh food is not lost on the customers.

This chapter discusses aesthetic generalities that affect the perception of the viewer toward the merchandise on the sales floor. Generic terms will be used here, such as light track, lamps or bulbs, instruments or lamp housing, sources or fluorescent (gasses lit inside a tube), and incandescent (the burning of a filament). Variations of those terms include halogen, quartz, HID, mercury vapor, etc.

There are several non-technical issues that should be understood to utilize lighting as a tool for directing the customer's eye to the merchandise. Within the confines of a selling space, they can be manipulated to produce predictable results. Every waking minute, we experience similar responses to changing light condi-

tions. The following topics in this chapter include the variables that comprise aesthetic responses.

The practical aspects of energy, heat, budget, and electrical codes are also discussed.

LIGHTING CONSIDERATIONS

- *Intensity and balance*
- *Focus or lighting position*
- *Color*
- *Daylight*
- *Heat*
- *Cost for installation and maintenance*
- *Decorative uses*
- *Theatrical (interior and windows)*

- *Energy use and legalities*
- *Intensity and balance*

Light levels need not be extravagant to achieve a comfortable viewing level, but consideration must be made to the entire space and all the merchandise before lighting should pick out feature items.

A light level that runs between 40 and 50 footcandles, or lumens (reflected light), or ambient light at merchandise level, is minimally reasonable to see all the merchandise. At this level, it is also possible to use a spotlight of the equivalent of 150 watts to punch out desired pieces of the presentation. There are lamps now that are use-rated at 75 watts with an output equal to the standard PAR 38, 150 watt lamp.

LIGHTING / PRICE CONNECTION

It is not the technical level of light in retail stores, but the perceived value to the merchandise that illumination intensity gives, that is critical. The lighting level described above says to the customer that a store is a mid-range shop, carrying good quality merchandise with a fashion tendency. When the level of light goes higher, the perception of the price, but not the value, drops. Higher light levels, reaching 80 and 100 foot candles, are very difficult to use if the desired effect is to highlight current trends. It basically signifies a shop that is carrying commodity items.

Even supermarkets that wish to project themselves as purveyors of fine foods along with staple grocery items will use a lower level of ambient light. Some use incandescent lights for produce, gourmet sections, and checkouts. Supermarkets such as Stew Leonard's in Connecticut and Byerly's in Minneapolis have sophisticated lighting systems that more closely resemble fashion stores than food shops. In Byerly's, lighting plays a large part in creating the transition for customers from the food sections to the store's fine jewelry and gift departments.

In higher-priced stores, the light level is generally lower, using primarily incandescent sources. Higher illumination levels tend to drop the perception of price, while lower levels will increase the perceived level of exclusivity. In either, the designer must maintain a minimum level of visibility and legibility for customers to see the merchandise and to read the signs. The comfort factor of lighting falls into a mid-range that prevents eye strain at both ends of the scale—too bright or too dim.

14.2

Harry Rosen, Toronto. There is a wonderful consistency of presentation for fine merchandise. Lighting in its simplest, most dramatic form is used to move the eye from display presentation to merchandise for sale.

(14.3)

**Potomac Mills,
Washington, D.C. All
malls should have the
ability to light store
fronts and
merchandise that is
put at the lease line.
This ability to move
and focus spotlights
can light the facade
sign of a temporary
tenant to bring it
closer to the mall
signing ethic of
quality.**

FOCUS

We previously discussed lighting positions that dealt with the use of the perimeter as an underutilized place for use of focusable spotlights. We also discussed valance lighting and the manner in which light hits the merchandise as a result of its proximity. In this section, the center floor and aisle lighting—the areas for most merchandise—is the topic.

The most unused place for light positions in specialty stores is directly in back of the facade. If the prime merchandise is thought to be in the front line of the store, a track can be focused on that merchandise. In most mall stores, there is a dead spot between the entry and the first merchandise to be viewed.

Even worse than this is when the mall merchant places fixtures at the lease line. This position gets no light from the store or from the center aisle of the mall. The merchandise is unlit and theatrically flat. Watch how customers will walk directly past this forward merchandise to the rack that has the first decent light. *All customers have an autonomic response to light.* Our eyes and then our bodies move to light.

Ceiling-mounted fluorescents on a grid pattern, whether flat or articulated, supply a minimum level of desired illumination to give sufficient ambient light so that all the products can be seen in a virtually shadowless environment. Some stores have used types of incandescent lighting, also in a grid, to add a color warmth to the general lighting. Other incandescents have been placed in "strategic" locations to give downlight.

In almost all instances these downlights do not have enough intensity to make a difference in illumination that is at merchandise height. When they do have the same effect, they generally hit the top of the merchandise in much the same manner as valance lights. Certain reflectors, both built into the lamps or in the housing, will make the beam of light narrow enough to use most of the lamp power to hit a small section of merchandise, but unless the lamp is focusable, the distracting effect of top lighting cannot be eliminated.

In a hardware/home fashion store in Guatemala, exposed fluorescent tubes were used for general illumination. For the price line and the fashion perception of the store this was correct. However, there never seemed to be enough light on the floor. The merchandise was shown in a space that was two stories high, with the lighting fixtures set at 24 feet. The solution was simple. Drop the fluorescent fixtures to 11 feet from the floor and re-lamp to get the maximum output with the same current being used. The store owner even changed the color of the bulbs, moving from a cool to a warm range, enhancing the home-like feeling.

In the center floor, the first issue of focus and lamp position is the departmental front row of merchandise, or Zone A. An easy way to handle this is to put a track in the center of the main traffic aisles. This will give a position to light either side of the aisle. Most spotlights are effective up to about 12 feet of the source. Mannequin arrangements and key merchandise presentations can be lit from this position.

The second area for general use of focusable spotlighting should be a ring around columns. Place the track about five feet from the cladding to illuminate the merchandise column. Light from this track can also be used for merchandise in the secondary aisles.

In a general merchandise store, if these two positions are covered, then there is a gap of between 20 to 30 feet between the center aisle track and the ring adjacent to the column. If another ring were placed between those two, now making the distance between two tracks no more than 12 feet, we could then attain maximum

flexibility and effectiveness to a permanently changing merchandise scene. It is not the installation of the track that is expensive, it is the initial provision for the power needed to supply all tracks at full capacity. As merchandise content and capacity shift, as the positions for display change, a flexible lighting position will pay off handsomely in the ease of placing a light where it will give higher illumination to the featured subject.

Multiple track positions are cost-efficient. They use a variety of standardized instruments of relatively low cost. A track system that gives flexibility to the placement of spots around the floor adds to the theatrical look of the area.

Emotions, Quebec.

Before: Merchandise displayed up to the lease line is an inefficient use of space. The items shown in that area are never lit, and block the entry into the shop.

After: As soon as the front racks were removed, and the merchandise was placed with other items spotlighted, customers came in.

(14.5)

Cemaco, Guatemala.

Before: This photo shows the height of the second floor ceiling and the height of the fluorescent fixtures off the ground level.

After: The banks of fluorescents were dropped from 24' to 11', creating a new visual ceiling. The re-lamping of the bulbs also gave a change of color, and better illumination per watt used. The increase in light intensity on the display and the focal point on the wall to move the eye from point to point. It does not hurt to have a secondary aisle that leads from the main traffic aisle.

COLOR

Lamps are rated by wattage and color. Daylight evokes a cool or blue-tone color, while lamplight, or incandescent, is on the warm side. The particular term for color range designation is Kelvin scale. The scale measures the temperature in degrees Celsius from absolute zero. Incandescent light is rated at 3200 degrees. Some fluorescents have also been developed to have the same rating. It is not only the lamp that can alter the perceived color on the floor, but also how that lamp color is reflected off the walls, the merchandise, and the customers. *Except for controlled circumstances, where the lamps are meant to fulfill a continued specific purpose, such as open frozen food cases, general ambient light color should be geared to give the most flattering effect to skin tones.*

Even now, with all the variety of equipment and lamps available, I find too many stores that have not adjusted the balance of their lighting for skin tones. If fluorescents alone were specified for a store interior, it is still possible to get this balance of color. Remember that lighting for RTW and home merchandise needs to be shown in the type of surrounding that customers will feel most comfortable when the product is taken out of the store. When customers see their skin tone take on a greenish hue because of the light, they may feel that the color of the garment or item does not match their personality.

DAYLIGHT

While sunlight gives most people a sense of well-being, just as cloudy days can make people dispirited, it is an uncontrollable light source for store interiors.

Stores facing onto the street in cities, strip mall stores, or regional malls, stores that open to a skylit atrium or have a window to the street, have the most problems in balancing the light at the entry or window to the light in the center and back of the shop. From the outside, daylight will create reflection. From the inside, the sun will visually bleach the color of the garment or package, and the ultraviolet rays will soon actually bleach the items.

Many customers who buy fabric or any RTW carry the merchandise to an outside window to check the color. In the fabric department of a French store, the management mounted a fluorescent fixture near the rack of fabrics and put letters on the fixture that read, "LUMIERE DU JOUR," meaning "daylight." Checking color

is a habit that will probably not be broken even though daylight causes the most variations in color and intensity. Designers should devise ways to use the positive effects of daylight from windows and skylights with minimum disruption to the controlled lighting areas.

14.6

M Store, Montreal. The overhead track and strut-frame system around the columns and in the center of the floor gave the designers many places to hang and focus their spotlights.

14.7

Printemps, France. The entire presentation is a beautiful sham. The third level of merchandise behind the hanging letters is a mirror reflection of the second shelf. The "Lumiere du Jour" (daylight) hanging fluorescent fixture is the ultimate deception, but it works.

(14.8)

A, B: Gantos, Michgian. The lighting coming from behind the timber frame valance did a marvelous job of lighting the walls. A piece of foamboard on the valance outriggers stopped the distracting light spill, held two forms of display, allowed a spotlight to be effective, and gave the department a new look. The top and bottom parts of the wall are the same color as they were before.

VALANCES

Initially, valances were designed to support tube lights that would evenly light, with high intensity, merchandise shown on the wall. When the direction of the valance light is focused down toward the item, the space above may be profitably used as a merchandise display or sign over the wall stock.

The edge of the valance is an excellent position for a strip of horizontal color or signing. The valance molding can be fitted with a snap-in strip to accommodate lamp sockets to accept Christmas lights.

With the same tubes that light the merchandise, designers can also construct the valance that is all backlit.

HEAT

All lights generate heat. The more focused a beam of light is, the more heat that it generates at the point of contact with an object. The build-up of heat is more of a problem for older downtown city stores than for newer suburban locations, or mall shops, where air circulation, ventilation, and air conditioning were part of the original planning. Older stores may have higher ceilings and operable windows to help dissipate the heat. Ceilings today are generally lower and the level of ambient light is more intense. Designers must provide a balance between the amount of light needed, the air cooling systems, and the comfort level on the sales floor.

Overly-hot dressing rooms.reduce try-on time and increase discomfort. For items that are tried on and rejected, retailers may have to deal with perspiration-stained garments.

COST FOR INSTALLATION AND MAINTENANCE

The most costly system to install is a complete light track system that accommodates low-voltage/high-intensity instruments. Equipment distributors claim a three-year payback. However, the cost of replacement bulbs is the highest. My objection to this system is the aesthetic effect. Small light fixtures are out of scale with a store's high ceiling height and the distance to the merchandise. A second problem is their lack of theatricality. The miniaturization of the light fixture detracts from the importance of the shape as an element in the design of the total space.

The least expensive installation is all- fluorescent. It also is the least expensive to maintain as bulb life is longer, and energy costs are down. The proportional cost of installation between the combinations of fluorescent and incandescent are equated to

their relative cost of maintenance. Many firms have adopted a re-lamping program to change all lamps on a set schedule, to reduce labor cost and illumination drop-off from aging of the lamps.

DECORATIVE USES

Lighting instruments used as an overhead border to define a space for a bank of counters are chosen as design elements and as sources. Jewelry counters can use many overhead point sources to illuminate the merchandise, as each lamp creates a new sparkle. These light fixtures are chosen to match the finish and the design of the counter units below. To merchandise their line of cosmetics, Clinique counters have special counter lamps to fit within their visual image.

Free standing floor and table lamps are generally not used for merchandise illumination, other than in a room setting, or in a special display. Customer safety is the main factor cited as the reason why stores do not use free standing lamps.

Chandeliers and wall sconces are effective for decorative effects and illumination. Fabricators can execute custom designs, or the designer can select from stock catalogs to meet the specifications of their store design.

THEATRICAL EFFECTS IN WINDOWS AND INTERIORS

Designers must provide the store's visual merchant with access to the most positions possible to set up a window display. In Chapter 8, we discussed hanging positions for mounting display materials, and the light track positions needed for windows. Since windows are fixed locations for presentation, the interior of the shop needs flexibility for displays.

For windows and interiors, designers should consider positions to light the presentation from all angles. Customers generally have no access to the display. Therefore there is no real concern for light in their eyes. Back, side, top, bottom, and front lighting give impact, and set off the presentation in a halo of light.

A designer can project a full year of presentation positions by selecting the place on the floor plan that is most likely in each department to get the first attention from customers. In that area, tracking and floor plugs can be preset (See Chapter 8). An overhead grid tracking system provides location flexibility. Some stores can drop an electrified track at desired intervals. Other stores may have portable wire grid systems that can make a mesh framework hold lamps and enclose a display in a type of proscenium.

ENERGY USE AND LEGALITIES

States have energy codes and each shopping center has criteria for energy use. Laws tend to be very conservative, and will cover the situation from the direst position. Designers generally use local contractors for their proximity to the project and for their knowledge of the local laws. Many correctly plan energy use on the safe side, and then add a dimension of protection.

Rising energy costs are a considerable portion of a store's operational budget. Designers and manufacturers are working together to improve the quality of light and keep the budget down. The designer's role is to find the right balance between the selection of the instrument, the installation, the cost of replacement, the compiled energy cost from the electricity used by the lamps, and the cooling units to keep the heat of the lamps in balance with the temperature of the room.

Henri Bendel, New York City. The chandelier was designed to move through the well and descend several levels. It can be trimmed to reflect the current merchandise stance.

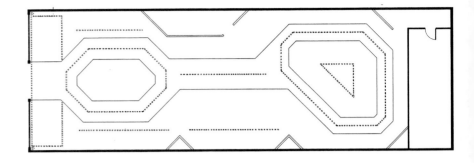

(14.10)

A: In a narrow store many wall positions can be lit from aisle tracking.

B: Hard aisles, columns, walls and windows are the key to position light track.

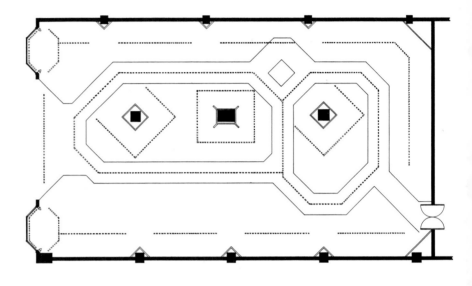

C: Continuing from the same key as above with one intermediate track.

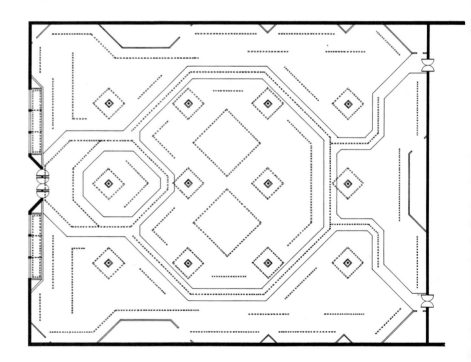

Chapter Fifteen

Departments Without Walls

t may seem that artists prefer to have no restrictions or limitations prior to starting a design project. However, there is always a sense of awe in facing a white canvas, or looking at a lump of clay that must be made into a creative entity. The same applies to a totally open space on a retail selling floor. Designers who shape the store must supply the tools for the visual merchandisers and merchants who present the merchandise on that floor.

Working with limitations can bring about a solution that is ingenious in its use of the space. Open selling spaces, without walls, elevations, or obstructions become a clean canvas that stretches the merchant's creativity. Although this type of space, or island department is generally associated with large stores, it can also occur in smaller specialty shops.

15.1

Nouvelle Galeries, France. This large (over 100,000 sq. ft.) branch store had virtually no way to stop customers' eyes from travelling to each outer wall. The decision to construct center floor storage in the cookware area permitted a multi-faceted structure whose sides were then the focus of prime sub-categories.

Many designers today are aware of the need to decrease the depth of selling areas from the aisle to the wall, and are putting in non-supporting walls that ring one or more of the loop traffic aisles. These walls are designed to be used from the inside of the loop and along the outer raceway. However, there are still many stores over 100,000 square feet that have no walls, except for the outer walls of the building. Whether small space or large space, the existence of an island department can be treated with the same integrity of design for merchandise as any department that has an enclosure. In this chapter the emphasis is on merchandise categories that do not use counters that are grouped as a selling island as their prime selling fixture.

WITH COLUMNS

When a defined open space contains a column it makes the task of locating the merchandise much simpler. Even when the column is not in the approximate center of the space, its height makes it the focus of the entire area. Most designers have done little or

nothing to use the interior columns for merchandise. The use of a clad column as a merchandise fixture can be designed and merchandised so that each of its sides represents a different merchandise sub-category. The sides of the clad column can be substantially larger than the basic structure supporting the building.

In Figure 15-1, the center of the column is used as a storage area for the department. The facia of the column unit is jogged in and out allowing for a presentation to show bulk items, and also splits off an item that has current sales desirability.

In Figure 15-2, the cladding around the column is the hub for wings that extend from the sides. The profile shape of these wings may be the same design as is prevalent in the department. They can be removed when not needed. The objective of the two treatments is to permit a high point in the center of the floor so that customers can locate the specific merchandise desired.

WITHOUT COLUMNS

When no column exists, and there is sufficient space on all sides to walk around, a dummy column may be installed. It is always better to align a dummy column with the architectural support columns, but it is not entirely necessary. Once merchandised, the column takes on a different look and customers do not recognize the discrepancy, even when the column does not touch the ceiling.

Figure 15-2 shows an unusual use of simple materials. Most stores already possess the basic materials to carry out this idea. Whether placed around and existing column, or put in free-standing space, this mirror-backed glass cube column holds an enormous amount of stock. It works best with china, glass, metallics, and small packaged items, including cosmetics. Rather than an obstruction requiring additional floor space to circumnavigate, the column is better used. In departments that measure over 30 feet square, there is no problem with its placement. "Drive aisles" from the main aisle get customers to move to the center of the floor. It works well, even if the column side is no less than four feet from the main aisle.

Specialty stores with a width of more than 25 feet can create an island in the center of the floor. This helps to create three main areas of merchandise presentation, and diverts traffic to the perimeter. There is then no strong center aisle to lead the eye past the first presentations.

There are few standard floor fixtures that have the capacity in height and width to be used as a center floor focus. There are screens that can be used as fixtures. That would be simi-

lar to constructing a dummy column.

Four shelving units can be placed in a cross at the center of the floor. Each wing of the configuration holds a different subdivision of items from the same category. This can be accomplished with RTW as well as shelved merchandise. The angle of the columns or fixtures should be 45 degrees to the main traffic aisle. This forces an angular presentation of the fixtures, making departmental access easier from the main aisle.

A series of platforms that serve as a base for a mannequin presentation, or a theatrical display can also elevate items, and stop the eye.

The issue of height will always be a factor to the merchant who wishes customers to see over every fixture. Height is fine, as long as the customers' interest is piqued to look around the merchandise or display. Customers do not stand still when shopping. Merchants should not judge a total presentation from one angle and simply say, "I can't see over it." Columns and high displays attract the eye, and properly presented can move merchandise faster than any other fixture in the assortment.

15.2

A. Kaufhof, Germany. The cladding around the column is already wide. The additions of the shaped wing walls gives greater product presence.

B. Loeb, Switzerland. The use of this glass cube column in the front of the department acted as a guidepost for the customers. A one-time increase in inventory led to increased sales and a far better sales-to-stock ratio.

OPEN SPACE

An open floor is like a sculpture waiting to happen. Sensitive designers and merchants can place fixtures and merchandise to move the eye up, down, and around merchandise.

An open space need not be a problem area. It can form the bridge between two strong perimeter presentations, or stand alone. Lighting helps to frame the space so that the area is visually contained. The combination of the additional impact of focus and increased intensity will direct customers' attention. Center floor positions help to reduce the depth of departments that run from the main aisle to the wall.

An open area can measure from 100 to 1,000 square feet. The use and the technical aspects are similar. The main differences are always in addressing the balance between the space, the merchandise depth, and the intent of the design.

Center floor positions have great flexibility. They may be used for promotion or display merchandise from all surrounding departments. They can link together adjacent departments, or to be a *swing area* for feature merchandise categories from two departments. A center floor can feature new arrivals. These areas without walls, because of their location in the traffic pattern, are a valuable assets to sellers.

The center of the store has a desirability that sometimes goes beyond the reality of its actual worth. When it is merchandised with the finesse needed to attract the eye and draw customers to examine the merchandise, it attains a greater value.

Not all space gets equal attention or equal sales. There will be hot spots that customers have tendencies to move towards, regardless of the merchandise. There are positions that customers walk past without giving a second glance regardless of the presentation excitement. The geography of the total selling space must work as a continuum of presentations that places merchandise in a sequence that respects customers' expectations, needs, and satisfaction.

Success of a total space provides a rhythm that uses open space, enclosed space, and adjoining aisles in harmony, creating an artistically acceptable, merchandise–adaptable presentation.

Chapter Sixteen

Remerchandising

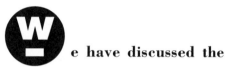e have discussed the role of designers when remerchandising requires a structural altering of the existing space. There is also a greater need to use designers to *remerchandise areas without making any physical structural changes.* Many of these changes must be accomplished without any capital outlay. How can designers contribute to the process of remerchandising? And, what is the process and the anticipated results?

WHEN TO CHANGE

The need to change the merchandise presentation in a store or a department stems from many different sources.

- *A change in the emphasis of inventory level to sales rate*
- *A new management team that wants to make its own mark*
- *An aggressive merchant who wants to appear current*

Each situation will mean an evaluation of space, fixturing, lighting, traffic patterns, and feature positions and merchandise.

Designers and visual merchants can play a key role in directing the remerchandising. I have found that most departments, their stock, their space, and their personnel can be repositioned with an ease that makes further changes seem almost effortless.

My staff and I have remerchandised stores of all sizes, all types of products, and in entirely different cultures. We have followed a process that accounts for the strengths of the company, yet falls into a determined pattern that has been resolved by using customer response as a basis. It has had consistently excellent results. We investigated the merchandise situation, planned the physical changes, primarily in traffic patterns, and

made note of needs for new fixtures or the best way to adapt older fixtures for new merchandise. In virtually every instance, the store already owned all the equipment needed to affect a change.

More than ever, when a change is being made in an existing area, and there are no contemplated staff changes, it is necessary to involve the staff in the decision-making process. This insures that they will take the responsibility to maintain the implemented changes. It gives them pride in ownership, and improves their sense of contribution to the selling of the items. This always translates into something called "sales-service." Should the staff not be involved with the remerchandising, and later questions about the presentation come up, it is a fairly sure bet that the staff will revert to the earlier presentation method where they feel safe.

A designer can recommend that a staff meeting be scheduled to explain the new merchandising format. Designers who run such a meeting should be as graphic as possible in the presentation. Use slides of past merchandise presentations, some from sister stores and some from competitors. Make diagrams on flip charts or on boards. Show optional methods of presentation, and ask which method the staff feels will work, and which one they will maintain.

If the goal of the remerchandising is logically explained, the response should be positive. If not, listen carefully to the reasons why. *The first-hand experience of the sales staff is the best marketing and operational information that you can get.*

FLOOR POSITIONING

For seasonal changes, consider floor positions for basics and off-price items. If the process for remerchandising that is outlined at the end of this chapter is adhered to, the department's staff will be able to carry out the tasks in the future with considerably less guidance. There are two primary issues to remember and use during this process.

1. *Sample the assortment*
2. *Step back to view the work in progress*

In every project where either of these steps has been neglected the results have been poor, and generally caused frustration.

THE SAMPLING PROCESS

The reasons for sampling become clear as the departmental repositioning evolves. First, take from the existing floor assortment one of each SKU. Different colors in the same style group are another SKU. Put a tag on them noting how many pieces exist on-hand. If there is less than a full size range, place the sample on another rack, or if it is packaged housewares, on another pallet. Those pieces in full range comprise the essential assortment.

When all sample pieces have been gathered, see which samples fit together by color, pattern, or style, within a reasonably similar price range. Color separation when apt, is the easiest to assemble and have customers see. The buying staff has anticipated hot items for the coming season, and these will fall into color, pattern, or style. This information must be part of the preparation process. Have the buyers point out the three key items in the assortment, and tell the staff why they bought them. They should explain which other items were bought to coordinate, which for fashion, and which for margin. *This information becomes the cornerstone to the placement of all the items in the department.*

Watch out for a department that has good, better, and best pricing on similar styles. I have found that the difference in price sometimes does not vary sufficiently in the mind of the customer to justify a different presentation format for the price separation, and that also includes many markdowns.

The sampling and the buyer's information will show where the strengths of the assortment are. It is always my preference to give feature space to those items that show strength by depth of quantity. However, if there is a need to go for a specific hot style, then the samples will permit the staff to select other items from the sample group which relate to and support the desired feature in a visually significant presentation.

For fashion items that are in broken size range within the first two weeks and still desirable, first try to coordinate them with similar items, and place them in with full mark-on items. Remember that there should be only one idea per fixture. If there are items that have sold well and are left on the floor with only one or two from the initial purchase, and will not be replaced, then they should be regrouped by end-use function. All tops, bottoms, etc., are placed on a round or straight rack, by size, and then colored within size. They need not be marked down. In fact, many European stores call this "End of Series" and customers know that these are the last pieces of best-selling items. Any item that is old, broken in size, or did not sell well, should be placed on another rack, by end use, sized and price marked. Where possible, try to group items of similar price and use the "two-fer" or "three-fer" system to move more

items more quickly. Their placement in the department plan is the last consideration following the setting of key and basic stock in full range.

Once the merchandise has been sorted and given trial designated areas, there is a constant need to step back from the department. *The first vantage point is taken from the direction of the customer flow. A second view could be from a ladder looking down onto the department.* The primary reason for both is to get a perspective, *an aesthetic distance,* from the merchandise. It is virtually impossible to get a good vista of the department while you are working in it. A view from floor level shows the elevations and leveling that leads the eye from feature to feature. Use a ladder. The high view is a great way to see the internal traffic aisle plan, and the spacing between the fixtures.

Samples should be used until all fixtures are laid out. Until the department is fully positioned with almost all of the samples in place, never bulk out the stock on the fixtures. Shifting a department that is fully stocked is a backbreaking problem that can be avoided.

Once a department has been reorganized and remerchandised completely, with sensitivity to the assortment, the display, signs, and lighting, expect the following to happen.

- *More customers come in to browse.*
- *More customers buy.*
- *Merchandise in the feature areas or at the focus points have very fast action. Sales velocity can jump from three to eight times.*
- *Holes in the assortment appear more rapidly.*

The latter occurrence is perhaps the greatest concern because the rate of sales can far exceed the norm. The success that you created may produce a poor reaction among customers who expect a fine presentation with an in-stock position. The preparation of the staff is worth the effort. If the area is remerchandised with staff who do not understand the process, the terminology, or the goals, a sense of participatory responsibility for maintenance will be lacking. I urge designers who are either on the store's staff, or who work for planning firms, to attend a departmental merchandising session. The learning experience is applicable to future problem-solving. It can liberate designers to spend more time with the touches that add visual personality.

21-POINT REMERCHANDISING CHECKLIST

The following 21-step list is the essential process to physically remer-chandise any category in any size area. They should be reviewed by project leaders before and during the process with the group; if adjustments are required, they will not disturb the basic sequence that gives the logic to the change.

1. **Have a plan! Know what your presentation goals are. Write them down.**
2. **Make sure that the area to be remerchandised and fixtures chosen are the right size for the stock that will be presented.**
3. **Sample the total assortment.**
4. **Strip the wall.**
5. **Clean all fixtures on the wall.**
6. **Select from the samples those items that have been given emphasis by the buyers. Select key wall areas for them.**
7. **With tape, lay out a traffic pattern of secondary aisles to those points on the wall. Set the tape from the primary entry point of the main aisle and lay out a path that visually and physically leads to those key items which have now become the focal points. Try to keep focal points in approximately a 45 degree sighting from the main aisle point of entry.**
8. **Reset the fixtures on the wall.**
9. **Place a sample of each item at the prime focal point on the wall. Start with the key items and then the rest by choosing those which best support the key item.**
10. **Step back. Check to see that the arrangement contains the items, is practical for self-service, and is aesthetically pleasing.**
11. **Strip the floor fixtures. Put all the remaining stock on rolling racks. Place floor fixtures along the tape borders that lead to the focal points. Adjust the fixtures to the size of the area and merchandise content.**
12. **Put samples on the floor fixtures to lead from feature to focal.**
13. **Repeat step No. 10.**
14. **Bulk merchandise the wall.**
15. **Repeat step No. 10.**
16. **Bulk merchandise the floor fixtures.**
17. **Repeat step No. 10.**
18. **Add props and signs if required. This is the time to add display and theatrical touches to create a feature presentation.**
19. **Focus the lighting.**
20. **Repeat step No. 10. Now enter the store and walk to the presentation simulating customer movement.**
21. **Make any adjustments that make the entire department more pleasing to the eye and easier to shop. You will probably have to readjust the positions of the floor fixtures to accommodate the content of each subdivision of merchandise, and clarify and straighten secondary aisles leading to the focal points.**

Before

Coin, Milan. Infant and Toddler. This project involved remerchandising 20 departments in four of the chain's stores in Milan. The mandate was to use the fixtures and the merchandise that already existed, and to train the store staff

After

to merchandise the new areas. The work was to be done over a three-week period. Speed, participation, correct interpretation from English to Italian, and vice versa, made the work one whirl of feverish activity.

After

This toddler department was particularly uninviting, due to the scale of the center floor shelving units. The ceiling was then painted pink to get a warm glow from the existing lights. The staff decided that a neutral color for the walls would be acceptable, and chose a no-color matte reflective mylar paper. The merchandise was placed on the wall first.

After

The small packaged items were put onto shelves. So much space was saved that a crib and mannequins were brought in to take up empty floor space.

Before

Coin, Milan. Women's Department. The combination of fixtures led to an impossible merchandising situation. Each fixture, including the wall, was quite well selected. But somewhere along the line, they got moved from one department to another, and subsequently misused.

Before

The variety of fixtures created a problem in setting the floor for the correct proportion of each sub-category.

After

Some of the fixtures were wood screens that got reused around the columns. Mannequins on platforms wearing the merchandise of the current season were placed around the columns. The jewel tones were on the left and the plaids on the right. The black section of wall was used to set off the yellow-beige grouping.

After

Entry from the escalator was considered, and aisle's were made to penetrate the department and separate the styles. During this early project we did not use tape to make secondary aisle delineation, but the checklist steps that were used here have been repeated in virtually all later departments.

Before

Coin, Milan. Men's Sweaters. If you study the before photo, you can see a brilliant cube system that was devised from "U" bend sheets of acrylic. The problem was that the differences in the price and the style of the items were inconsequential to the fixturing. Note that the back wall cubes were not filled and the lighting was flat.

After

The only added item to this presentation was a set of graduated cubes to hold bust forms. The merchandise on them was the new argyle V-necks. The rack on the right held promotionally priced items. The back wall was divided by lambs wool and cashmere followed by a separation by V-neck, crew neck, and cardigan.

After

Mirrors were placed for customers to see themselves as they either held the sweater against their chest, or tried it on. An amazing thing happened in this self-service area. The customers took out the sweater, and if it did not suit them,

After

they refolded it and put it back. I produced a set of photos to show the incredulous management that customers do respect a neat presentation. Their jocular response was, "Those that refolded were Swiss, not Italian."

Before

M Store, Montreal, Place Versailles. Children. The mandate was, "Save the chain, or we close." The original merchandising mentality of the company was steeped in supermarket presentation techniques derived from their parent company, Steinbergs. Mangagement lost confidence in its staff, and morale was low. The visual attitude was

After

based on a "me too" of who was successful. That year it was the Target stores. By looking at the decor rather than the entire marketing/ merchandising strategy, they did not stand a chance. Strangely, the best merchandising was done in the stockrooms where corporate policy had not reached.

After

The managers of the stores placed their reserve stock in a sequence that made sense for them to locate, but were actually prohibited from using the same intellect to put out the stock for customer selection. The theme for the project became, "Let's make the stores look like a fashion warehouse."

After

When the merchandising teams had their aesthetic sensitivities released, they found a new pride in their work. Customers could not believe that it was the same store. Within a year the assortment was adjusted to show new customer interest. The sales increased, and the percentages of soft goods to hard goods shifted from a 30 - 70 percent opening split to a year end 55 - 45 percent split.

Before

M Store, Montreal. Women's and Men's. The first photo shows the store in transition. The next three are mens' and womens' departments that were designed and executed with the existing staff.

After

The follow-thru was so complete that the company developed merchandise specialists who would work in the field doing the presentation with the staff, and then report back to the buyers to consult with them on the quantity needed and most applicable styles for each store's assortment.

After

Columns, walls, and aisles became most important. Training teams dedicated themselves to teaching this to floor merchandising staffs.

After

When the remerchandising was all over, the management could again look to the future with positive planning. At the conclusion of the entire project, the director said, "We had one advantage over the competition. We were desperate!"

Before

Kitchen Bazaar, Rockville, Maryland. Coffee Makers.
A neat but insignificant coffee presentation without focus to
the wall.

After

The pyramid group of the coffee makers now with a clear
vista to the coffee mugs on the wall. The coffee mugs are
the number one unit seller in this department.

Before

Kitchen Bazaar, Rockville, Maryland. Cookware.
Before remerchandising, the company put almost all
cookware on the wall. This created horizontal merchandising
that used zone A, B, and C for seperate merchandising
categories.

After

The remerchandising focused the wall on the key cookware
grouping and brought the other support groupings forward,
now leading the eye from the aisle feature presentation to
the focal point on the wall.

Before

Johnston & Murphy, New York City. A review by company executives of this business/comfort-related men's shoe chain accurately stated that "The quality of the window presentation does not come up to the quality of the merchandise." The cube presentation was done without consideration for the customer's need to see each group separately.

After

A desk was used with related props to vary surface levels and to imply a relation to the office. However, the starting point for the presentation was the lighting, not the desk. Each group of shoes in the "after" picture is lit with a low-voltage high-intensity desk lamp. Desks became a necessary adjunct to the clarity and drama of the presentation.

Before

Steinbach's, Connecticut. The purpose of this re-do was to introduce a new house branded shirt.

After

With very little expense and a lot of good sense, virtually all the old fixtures were used. It is amazing what a bit of stained molding can accomplish around a glass cube.

Before

Eastern Mountain Sports, New Hampshire. Lots of merchandise shown without rhythm takes time away from shoppers who wish to find a specific item and then may do some browsing and impulse buying.

After

The kayak above the Patagonia unisex merchandise is placed at the center of the far wall between the men's and women's categories. The eye shape attracts eyes. The compacting of end-use items presented in critical masses, gives a focus to the department and allows space to do coordinate presentations.

Before

Eastern Mountain Sports, New Hampshire. Backpacks. The "Before" presentation was the standard until a few questions were asked- "How do you sell them, and how do your customers buy them?" This led to the following observations:

1. EMS sells more backpacks than any other store chain.
2. It is a heritage item, a destination for many shoppers.
3. Only the day packs and the fanny packs are self-service.

After

4. All other packs, from camping to mountain climbing, are fitted by a trained salesperson.

The staff then decided to make a full sample display of all the different types and colors in stock, and put the excess in the stockroom. After a selection was made the salesperson asked, "Would you prefer a fresh one from stock?" Presentation and service went hand in hand.

Before

J. Byrons, Florida. Men's. A standard, flat, academic presentation.

After

With little addition (the column and the lighting) the same area was converted. When spotlights did not exist at the front of the department, the mannequins were moved to the wall. The spots at the back of the column were turned to focus on the mannequin group.

Before

J. Byrons, Florida. Don't let anyone tell you that "grid pattern" merchandising can put more goods on the floor. All it can really do is create a boring, unbroken, difficult to merchandise, and anti-sales department.

After

The use of secondary aisles with the columns is the key to making an area responsive to artistic, pragmatic, serviceable sales.

Before

Color Tile, Huntington, New York. These stores were part of a chain that belonged to the Tandy Corporation. The store catered to contractors and do-it-yourself customers.

Before

However, the presentation gave no consideration to multiple ideas for the novice, nor did it create an atmosphere that was being put forth by many of its competitors.

After

The remerchandising followed the same principles as RTW. Get the traffic flowing to prime merchandise. Use stacks of boxes in an intelligent, aesthetic presentation on the floor, and feature the high margin accessories at the end of the shopping trip. One cautionary note...when setting boxes of

After

floor tiles, have a plan, don't guess. The staff was so happy to see that their work areas permitted visual excitement, that they made beautiful mosaic panels to show off the different types and colors of tiles.

Chapter Seventeen

Coordination—Support Systems

VISUAL MERCHANDISING, MARKETING, ADVERTISING AND PROMOTION

The technical objective of store design is to turn abstract space volume into retail selling space by applying the designer's skills to create a visual reality. Designers take the information given to them by the merchants and the operations staff, described in the information gathering process in Chapter 6, and convert the words into pragmatic aesthetics. During this process, designers conceptualize the movement of customers from the beginning to the end of the shopping trip. The result of their design efforts should aesthetically fulfill customers' expectations before they enter the store itself. Yet, with all the prior interviewing that occurs with the central staff, the designer needs to visualize the store as an entity with distinct characteristics given it by the marketing, sales promotion, visual merchandise and the advertising teams.

They have the responsibility to formulate the policies that input the image that the store's CEO has established. The attitudinal and pragmatic aspects of the store design process are welded at this juncture. Structural choices have already been determined. At this stage, the selection of colors, materials, and finishes is made. It is time to select the wood, carpet, marble, metal, papers, tile, and paint colors that will balance customers' quality perception to the visual actuality.

The designer must coordinate at all decision-making levels, from the CEO through the entire company's organization chart. It is important to include the store's staff, including the entire visual team. Each specialty will support each other specialty; the end result will be to bring the merchandising effort to life at the point-of-purchase.

TIMING

A store opening is most time consuming. After opening, as the merchandising cycle starts, the process of changing presentation and interdepartmental communication speeds up. Eventually the cycle will contain major events and minor promotions. From fully-planned starting capacity, to merchandise that seasonally changes, to internal boutiques, all of the departments will have a role to play and a product or service to deliver.

The task of converting the merchant's wish list into reality takes talent and political finesse. The valuable information to be given to designers from the marketing, advertising, sales promotion, and visual merchandising departments is the spice that adds the flavor to the guts of the design.

MARKETING

The information provided by the marketing director has two purposes:

- *Define products that appeal to those customers who best represent their potential clientele.*
- *Define your customer base to increase the productivity of the store.*

The marketing director has information and historical records with which to make projections. The ages, mobility, desires, habits, and patterns of customers become a fabric on which the retailing table is set.

Merchants get information about customers from the marketer for interpretation into style, price, and need. They support policies that are experimental and may also follow hunches that are set in motion by separating a trend from a fad.

However, research and past history generally prove to be the basis for determining which purchases, store position, pricing, and presentation will give retailers a unique position in the mind of their clientele.

Intellect and risk taking are part of the marketer's venue. Forethought, communication, and planning make their work a shared experience.

ADVERTISING

Once the customer has been defined and the merchandise selected, the advertising manager determines how best to get the company's message into the marketplace so that the advertising investment is returned by enticing more people into the store.

Advertising managers select media best suited to reach the most potential customers. They know what radio stations, newspapers, and T.V. channels their targeted customers use regularly. They place the ads at a time when most customers pay attention. The information from the marketing department indicates when most customers drive to work and listen to the radio, watch prime time network news, read tabloids or financial pages, read books or magazines, spend time on the job or are homemakers. Ads will run in series or as a timed blitz. Ad budgets are established as a percentage of sales. The campaign includes using all applicable aspects of advertising and in-store merchandise coordination.

Retail advertising professionals can fairly well predict the numerical response to any ad campaign, both in dollars and in units. Their primary job is to bring people to the store and then let promotion and presentation guide the shopper to the product.

Advertising media are primarily seen outside the store. Ads can also be shown in a department, either mounted into a frame , or shown on a video monitor. Another effect on the physical layout occurs when a major ad announces a special short-term sale. Customers line up outside of each entrance and flow in as the doors are opened.

I have seen stores adjust their fixtures and widen their aisles to permit a literal race of customers into the store. Special signs need to be placed to direct traffic and to locate designated sales areas. Rack, counter, and overhead signs are used for product and price emphasis. When plans have been made earlier for these events, the store need not take on the look of an unmanaged and devalued barnyard. Loyal customers will not be turned off if the sale is conducted with the same intelligence that is exhibited at non-sale periods.

PROMOTION

Sales promotion focuses more on direct mail than in-store visuals. However, it still resides mainly with this department to unify the visual approach taken by catalogs, mailers, and in-store presentation.
The wording for price and announcements is also generated by the sales promotion department, and the

strongest linkage made is between advertising and visual merchandising. Communications from all departments must convey exactly the same message about the store and its image to the customer.

VISUAL MERCHANDISING: IN-STORE MARKETING

Visual merchandisers were formerly referred to as "display directors." In department stores, their responsibility was to glamorize those items in the show windows which best represented the current fashion stance of the store. In fact, the word "window" has been used to designate the profession of display in other languages. In France, they were called *etalagists*, or people whose concern was the shelf behind the window glass. In Germany, *schaufenstermacher*, or show window maker, and in Italy, more directly to the point, they were and are still sometimes called *vitrinisti*, or window people. Today, display professionals who work in a retail store prefer to be called "visual merchants" and most languages freely adopt the words from English.

In the past, some display departments selected merchandise for the windows based on their own tastes, even though the items shown were not in size range in the department, or worse, were the only ones in the store. Yet this practice persisted in many stores because the draw of the display presentation outweighed the intermittent customer annoyance at not finding an item that was "advertised." The power of presentation led many retailers to upgrade the position of Display Director to Visual Merchandising Director.

The additional responsibilities of display were also matched by the increase in the number of stores under the same name. As the importance of regional malls grew to the profitability of the company, the importance of walk-in street traffic and window display decreased. Display specialists were asked to extend their window magic into the store itself.

FROM WINDOWS TO IN-STORE VIGNETTES

Now, they turned their talents to vignettes on the aisles, using the same mannequins, props, and techniques that they used in the windows. However, the transition required a greater knowledge of the merchandising process than they previously had to consider. *The display now had to relate to the merchandise for sale on the sales floor.* This added responsibility correctly spawned the idea that the visual merchant could either add to, or actually take the responsibility for store planning.

As these new functions developed, the display teams went to market with the buyers. Terms such as critical mass, which were once used exclusively by marketers and store leasing agents, found their way into the jargon of the visual merchant. They started assembling merchandise on the floor in conjunction with the displays to create an in-store advertisement. As such, their aesthetic sensitivities were used to judge the amount of stock needed to maintain the image of value that the store merchants wished to express, even if that meant camouflaging stock shortages. From the initial impact that the visual merchant had in the windows, where their work was to present, stop, entice, and direct customers, they now took the new responsibility of assisting in the sales of that merchandise.

Today, with the change of merchandising that has brought us huge, centrally controlled specialty stores, super category stores, shopping centers, and manufacturer controlled retail, visual merchants are asked to train colleagues and tenants in the aesthetics of presentation. *Retail companies that have made the strongest transitions over the past 50 years have also maintained the strongest visual merchandising principles.*

A PROPER MIX

Shifts of tastes in decor and in fashion style are a guide to the chronology of design. Stores that project specific current trendy styles date themselves as quickly as consumer tastes in fashion and design change. When architectural formats do not permit style change, the architecture becomes more important than the items for sale. *When the architecture wins, the merchandise loses.*

A proper mix of the store's design takes into consideration that the entire structure will be compatible with:

- *changing product styles*
- *the scale of the space*
- *merchandise presentation in a setting that does not fight the intent of the products*

I have seen many examples of stores where the design was overpowering. When asked to remember the most outstanding characteristic of the store, customers would say, "The beautiful staircase."

There are also store designs that attempt to fix the presentation by designing very clever and currently correct merchandising units. Merchandise styling, however, has never remained static. Attempts to externally regulate fashion needs do not last. Even banks today adapt their space format to the changing styles of customer needs; they have become retailers in displaying and packaging financial services.

Rebuilding and renovating represent considerable capital expenditures. It is more cost-efficient to complement the store design with strategically placed, appealing, image-driven, changing display and presentation. Utilizing the visual merchandising team as the in-store marketing arm of the company will provide benefits that are translatable into productivity.

A UNIFIED MISSION STATEMENT

The process of information gathering and resultant presentation for customer acceptance is a means of bringing home a singular message. Designers as part of this support team must see how other groups create space needs.

- *The marketer's analysis of customer's aspirations is translated by designers into construction materials and ambience.*
- *Advertising creates a need to buy which determines the balance of space between the merchandise and the width of the passages.*
- *Sales promotion influences sales in catalogs and in in-store events that gives designers the keys to the ambience of departments.*
- *Visual merchandising programs floor presentations, off-floor storage, and/or work areas.*
- *Special events, public relations, training, and personnel all support the selection within the stated mission of the company.*

Designers put together plans that augment the advice given by each department head. As the cycle of the seasons progresses and the needs of the retailer change, the initial design of the store should have the flexibility to absorb change and still maintain a consistent visual image.

Chapter Eighteen

Specialty Leasing

CARTS, KIOSKS, AND TEMPORARY TENANTS

Designing for self-sufficient selling units has become a whole new sub-category of retail design and merchandise presentation. The direction of the retail industry and the shape of selling space has irrevocably changed, and is continuing to change. Among these changes is the new importance of specialty leasing–carts, kiosks and temporary pre-fabricated stores–and it is one of the fastest growing segments of the retail industry. Understanding the reasons that brought about this growth aids in implementing its potential.

The entrepreneurs who open these shops evolved from radical adjustments in the retail industry. They bring with them new products, new ideas, and a vitality that incorporates a freshness of approach for the individual sellers and for retail developers.

(18.1)

(left) Fanueil Hall Marketplace, Boston. The original festival marketplace combined restoration and old-fashioned merchandising with products brought to market by a wider variety of merchants than could be found in standard malls. It succeeded because it attracted locals on a regular basis, and became a prime tourist spot. Cart development has become a major business as a result of this early, forward-thinking market.

(right) Union Station, St. Louis. Between two shopping centers is a passage that clusters carts so that no shopping opportunity or space is wasted.

In an economic climate when conservatism in buying is coupled with the need to attract shoppers, very interesting solutions emerge that will hold a key position for future long-range planning.

The decade of the 1980's which witnessed a dramatic shift in the core business of retail may be tame when balanced against projections for the 1990's, and beyond to the year 2000. As selling and merchandise spaces change form, as the cycle of retail maturity accelerates, old ideas get recycled and initiate truly new innovations. New configurations of shopping centers, new types of stores, (the wholesale warehouse club, for example, and free-standing single category stores such as Toys-R-Us) changed the pattern of thinking about contiguous retail relationships.

During the 1980's, independent single unit owners and mid-range chains were hurt most by the changes caused by global retail problems. These changes included:

- *The shape and cost in space rentals*
- *Consolidations in store ownership*
- *Dwindling manufacturing resources from which to chose*
- *The increase in the cost of doing business*

For many of the surviving small retailers and independent chains, the main goal has shifted from the business of retail merchandising to debt restructuring, retail financing, and real estate management. The speed of decision-making and communications has altered their timing and their perceptions of creative retailing. Finance now controls the attention of virtually every retailer. Business buyouts and failures showed that the retailers had convinced everyone and themselves that their businesses were undervalued. Undervaluation of the retail organization reflected on the profession. In a survey of business school graduating classes retail was twelfth of thirteen choices of desired professions to enter.

The managers and owners of small chains and the new entrepreneurs who were encouraged by the sales generated by the economic environment of the 1980s became merchants who now form the nucleus of the specialty operations.

Concurrently, the fastest-growing segment of the entire retail industry (but not fiscally larger than the warehouse clubs) is specialty leasing. It is no coincidence that visual merchandising by the developer team contributes greatly to the success of the specialty industry, because of the knowledge and use of sophisticated presentation techniques. *Specialty leasing deals with carts, kiosks, wall, and temporary tenants in shopping centers.* A new staff position in many mall organizations is Vice President for Specialty Leasing.

The use of the center court common area for selling merchandise has spawned new industries in portable fixture design. Carts and kiosks add to general traffic, and encourage additional visits from loyal shopping center customers, and everyone benefits. What are these specialty merchandise sales mini-environments, and how do they affect the design and traffic flow of the mall?

CARTS

There is an historic association to cart sellers in every culture. Even today, on the street, in transportation terminals, in stores, and in shopping centers, carts represent an aspiring entrepreneur. The shopper perceives finding an item from a unique source, with value. Guaranteed to have face-to-face, close contact with the seller, the buyer has many expectations. What they seek is similar to the expectations of customers prior to entering a traditional selling space. The carts used by The Rouse

Company, one of the most innovative center developers, when assembling the parts for Boston's Faneuil Hall, became a symbol of the future "festival marketplace" genre. These centers were often reconstructions in historic locations that became increasingly important in the rebirth of faltering city centers.

Carts represent an investment on the part of developers. They are nurturing a new concept along with the retailer. Carts enjoy the potentially most productive space in the shopping center with a full traffic flow. Many carts can show sales of $1,000 per square foot.

Carts are bought and owned by the developer. They come equipped to present and sell most types of merchandise, and can easily be adapted for unique items. They have virtually no start-up costs, and are the least expensive way to get a place in a high-traffic mall. The mall installs the phone lines and cash terminals in cart positions.

18.2

Marche de la Ouest, Montreal. This farmers market was conceived as an open air produce market. The vendors were encouraged to prepare their food for consumption in an adjoining closed area. Carts and small retail shops became an accessory to the food business. The Marche is still a major draw in Montreal, and has encouraged many other retail developments to be constructed around the area.

18.3

Copley Plaza, Boston. Modular construction makes for easy installation of these units. Note the 45 degree angle of the facades. Isn't it easy to read the names of all the shops? Why aren't more mall "streets" designed that way?

Carts are designed to be self-sufficient selling units. They can be refrigerated, heated, lit, and wheeled to the next propitious location. For some merchandise categories, they are difficult to merchandise and display, but creative cart merchants work with the same devices that major stores use for setting floor stock. Some cart vendors who sell merchandise that is fairly small can store it within the unit. For other categories of merchandise, the mall provides stock storage space.

Carts can be custom made to accommodate the image and special needs of the retailer and the developer. Developers have an opportunity to regain a unified visual aesthetic for their centers by encouraging cart merchants. They are an effective draw for such events as the opening of a new center or wing, or major renovation.

Developers who have invested in carts for their center rent them for a percentage of the sales, plus a monthly minimum. This percentage is higher than in-line stores, and is justified by little, or no, start-up cost. Some cart owners are new retailers and need to be nurtured. Developers and merchants can determine whether the embryonic cart businesses go in a different direction, such as permanent kiosks or in-line permanent stores. The developers are incubating their own retailers.

Some cart businesses are nationwide. This is also true with kiosks and temporary tenants. In these operations, the presentation will be managed from a central control. These are businesses whose product has a short but profitable life span. Some "temporaries" have worked out leases beyond a single year. Cart design has become a new aspect of store design. The forms are basic and limiting. The cost per cart is fair for the manufacturer, the developer, and the retailer. Size limitations push the creative energy to be innovative, not merely clever.

KIOSKS

Kiosks are generally four-sided, freestanding shops. They may have counters or walls to define the shape of the space. Walls are often seethrough. Kiosks hold considerably more stock than carts and require additional sales staff on busy days. Developers have used kiosks to change traffic patterns.

Malls have set very high design criteria for kiosks. The materials used, and the stylish appearance make many of the kiosks better-looking and more profitable than in-line stores selling the same category.

Kiosks are mostly self-contained, including track lighting. Some malls have provided center court spotlights to further illuminate the shopping space. Kiosk manufacturers are producing some exciting new fixtures for a new era of merchandising

WALL SELLING

Some passages and walls in center court areas that are now being used as an important background for merchandise. The importance of the wall as a prime selling area was previously covered. It holds the same importance in the merchandising schemes for the center court.

Virtually any selling device can be used to show merchandise against a wall. Most malls that use the wall space use one or both of the following design ideas:

- *Built-in shallow shops that can house merchandise in a front counter and on the wall.*
- *Open shelving units. Even RTW items use a folded merchandising system with a few face-hung garments in order to hold more stock and tell a story.*

Since it is a wall position, the vendor has an ability to go higher than freestanding units. The developer should provide a device to use the height for either signing or merchandise.

The value of carts and kiosks is being recognized by the shopping center merchants. Many large and small in-line stores, including the anchors, are renting center court space to use as outposts for hot-moving merchandise on a seasonal basis.

Mall of Memphis, Tennessee. The farmers market has been brought inside, under the cover of the mall. Food is the primary item sold in a mall, whether it is to be eaten on the premises, or taken home.

IN-LINE TEMPORARIES

Empty stores on a street or in a mall threaten the retail survival of the area. When vacancies occur, other tenants become frightened, and the entire selling area loses credibility. Mall developers use several effective techniques to cover the holes. For example, decorative masonry blocks or attractive graphics conceal the empty store from the public. But all of this is only camouflage, and does not fool shoppers for long.

When the life of a center is threatened by vacancies, developers have turned to a formula called a "vanilla box." They create a shell, using basic fixturing that can accommodate both shelving and hanging stock. The mall team then helps with the signing and the merchandising, and gets the store operating quickly without normal start-up construction costs. Most of these vanilla boxes are simply covering the walls with fixtures. Excellent concept though it is, the mall developer's designers should provide some way to break the long wall presentations into smaller chunks. Movable partitions or triangular prisms on casters can be placed at any point along the wall to help group a single merchandise style statement.

The lighting system uses both incandescent track lights and fluorescent. The general effect has shown that new merchants can quickly get their units open and operating, and look quite presentable to shoppers.

DEVELOPER'S PROFIT OPPORTUNITY

These are new areas for retail designers. It is fairly certain that this industry called "specialty leasing" will be around for a while. Developers who once thought that they could open a shopping center and manage it on the basis of space sales alone are now learning that they must also be merchants, and be in charge of the retail packaging of their properties. As such, they look for new ways to hold and increase their markets.

Developers are a new breed of retailer, buying services and fixtures once exclusively produced for store owners. They have a healthy respect for design in their centers and have a vested interest in the continuation of their sales growth. Designers who can see this relationship, and can adjust for the scale, will have one more avenue for their services.

Chapter Nineteen

Evaluation Techniques

tore design and visual merchandising have a responsibility to the bottom line of the company. Their activities have a direct and indirect effect on profitability. The function of design is to create the ambience that makes shoppers buy more and buy more often. This book focuses on understanding what design can do to produce imagery that generates expected responses. It is also about the shared experience in setting priorities that respect the intelligence of the staff, and the customers. The effects of visual merchandising and store planning are measurable and accountable.

Although sales figures are a result of combined efforts, I would still insist on record-keeping for the following statistics. They give a clear picture of the action in the store, and where it is happening.

1. *What is the percentage of purchasers to the number of customers entering? This is called "sales penetration."*
2. *How many items were bought for each purchasing visit? Merchants refer to this as "add-on purchasing."*

A history of these numbers will surely show a response to any completed renovation.

I stress item count over value. Markdowns and clearance sales can produce a high volume, and low or no profit. Increasing unit sales deals with the susceptibility of that market to purchasing any item. It also give a more consistent picture, less any unusual promotions, to see the selling floor as the *prime* selling media. Because it must respond to momentary changes in the purpose of the assortment, the use of the selling space is more flexible than radio, television, and print.

Any evaluation requires an objectivity that also means judging the qualities of your own creation. Many times we are too harsh with our own and more lenient with others. Evaluations produce information that is both laudable and treatable. There are guides to visual effectiveness that invariably parallel financial evaluations. Questions may be altered to fit particular needs. Intuition is a good a guide for composing the questions.

This evaluation checklist was used in a course given to the mall managers, marketers, and leasing agents of the Hahn Company, a major shopping center developer, during their Hahn School seminars. The numerical results that they obtained graded the visual impact of the stores. The percentile ratings were exactly scaled to the store's profitability and productivity. When they presented their findings they used terms that gave them a new credibility as visual merchants.

The checklist has been used to evaluate all types of stores selling all varieties of merchandise. If there are items not applicable, then subtract their value from the total before beginning, and restructure the percentage base. The result is: design has a direct effect on sales.

The following checklist can be used by merchants and designers to rate their store against the competition. Arrive at a percentage grade by adding up all applicable points (5 points for each item) and then dividing that total into the total of your scores for those items.

Here is the way to judge your score:

- *Over 90%. You will probably exceed projections.*
- *80% to 90%. Doing well, better than others in the field.*
- *70% to 80%. Cautious but steady, reliably average sales.*
- *60% to 70%. Inconsistent, possible problems.*
- *50% to 60%. Slow decline seen, call for help.*
- *40% to 50%. Major problems.*

The points that you give to each item are based on the following rating system. Your immediate response is all that is needed. Trust your judgement and intuition.

- *5 points: Maximum for a memorable, outstanding job.*
- *4 points: Effective and inviting.*
- *3 points: Attractive, but just sits there.*
- *2 points: Amateurish.*
- *1 point: No effect, waste of time.*
- *0: Wrong image, counterproductive*

	Store One	Store Two
Shopfront:		
1. Does it reflect the company purpose?		
2. Is it well maintained?		
3. Is the store sign legible?		
Windows:		
4. Clear story?		
5. Merchandise story current?		
6. Is the space well kept?		
7. Are the items shown lit from the front?		
8. Are the signs well used?		
9. Is there an idea being sold?		
10. Is it (are they) imaginative?		
Entrance:		
11. Inviting, not cluttered?		
12. Three or more categories visible?		
13. Clear routing (traffic pattern) to areas?		
Interior Center:		
14. Categories clear?		
15. One category, one fixture?		
16. Fixtures grouped for adjacent coordination?		
17. Fixtures related to the wall merchandise?		
18. Lighting - sufficient level?		
19. Lighting - highlighted features?		
20. Store color - does it work for the merchadise?		

	Store One	Store Two
Interior Wall:		
21. Is it visually rhythmical?		
22. Does it tell a specific merchandise story?		
23. Are there clear, high focal points?		
24. Is it shoppable?		
25. Does the focal point contain the same merchandise that is in the feature presentation		
Fixtures:		
26. Are fixtures the right size for the assortment?		
27. Are they in good repair?		
Merchandise:		
28. Well-balanced for the cubic space?		
29. Appears to be a full choice of each range?		
Signing:		
30. Are the signs legible?		
31. Is there a good use of words		
32. Is the message clear ?		
33. Non-redundant to the merchandise ? Do the words tell something that is not evident in seeing the item ?		
34. Encourages one or more purchases?		
35. Manufacturer's identity clearly indicated?		
36. Are the graphics in keeping with the advertising?		
Cash-Wrap:		
37. Counter top cleanliness?		
38. Back counter neatness?		
39. Accessibility of items for sale?		
Staff:		
40. First impression?		

The customer is always right!

They look right, turn to the right, move to the right, and start forward motion with the right leg. Because of our physical being, this right orientation happens so frequently that customer behavior is predictable. They respond in patterns that can be controlled. *Retailers control the space in their stores and subsequently control the response and level of acceptance of their customers.*

Throughout history, marketplaces in every culture used the control of the senses to seduce, lure, or entice shoppers by setting a selling atmosphere. Aroma is mixed with the sound of selling and buying. The visual delight of merchandise, always on display, presents itself to combine with touch for sensory verification. Savory delights link with aromas to reinforce the transmission of sensory messages.

Creating the proper framework to enhance the potential purchase is the prime work of retailers and their designers. It is a serious game that is played to convince prospective customers that what is for sale is desirable and selling at a fair market value.

Creating the store in accordance with the known and anticipated behavior of its patrons makes overwhelming sense. Using this knowledge as a basis, a logical springboard, permits designers to shape a space to the unique image established by the company.

There are many merchants who properly use principles of a formal retail behavioral study in an intuitive manner. But few merchants have made and used studies of behavioral patterns to deliberately employ the combination of sensory stimuli and physical customer tendencies.

MERCHANTS' PRIORITIES

A retailer's first priority is to make the store's customers feel content—with their purchase, the time that they spent making it, and the manner in which it was bought. High customer comfort levels are achieved when all elements of merchandising, store design, and presentation continuously work in synchronization.

In this book, I have tried to humanize the process of design thinking for retail store layout and merchandise presentation. Customers and store personnel have habits, values, and information that must be respected. When the words "customer driven" are used to defend a design process, they should mean more than just jargon. True customer-driven design need not exclude the personality of the retailer or the designer, *but should first identify the customers level of comfort and their degree confidence in the credibility of the store.* Design creativity takes the given of the customer's needs, and layers that with the aesthetic desire to fulfill the retailer's image, both visual and practical.

The information in this book puts words to images. Aesthetics becomes the basis for visualization of a selling area. Merchandise is the first presentation consideration, but still only a part of the entire picture. Logic is stressed over formula, and if nothing else works, the intuitive response is perfectly acceptable. The definitive evaluation is, "Is the merchandise selling?" If the space works, it is a good design solution.

In an industry where change is the lifeblood of sales, it is wise to look for one position from which to understand the speed of change. For me, that position will always be the customers. In their intellectual responses to changing styles in business, living, and dress, they are reasonably certain to physically respond in a manner that is historically predictable.

Customers want to trust retailers, and will go to extra efforts to purchase merchandise from merchants they relate to. Designers can make it easier for customers to shop intelligently, save time, and find gratification in their purchase.

The objective of *Design For Effective Selling Space* is to bring to the attention of designers and merchants new insight and knowledge regarding customer response to the physical elements of a selling area. Some industry observers have said, "Merchandising is a combining of the science of retail with the art of design." From my experience, the opposite is true. Design and presentation are the sciences, while merchandising is the art. I hope you agree.

Bibliography

Ackerman, Diane. *A Natural History of the Senses*. New York: Random House, 1990.

Anderson, Patricia M., and Leonard G. Rubin. *Marketing Communications*. Englewood Cliffs, New Jersey: Prentice-Hall, 1986.

Brillat-Savarin, Jean Anthelme. *The Physiology of Taste*, trans. M.F.K. Fisher. New York: First Harvest/HBJ, 1978.

Campbell, Joseph, with Bill Moyers. *The Power of Myth*. New York: Doubleday, 1988.

Cash, R. Patrick, Editor. *The Buyer's Manual*. New York: National Retail Merchants Association, 1979.

Cialdini, Robert B. *Influence*. New York: Quill, 1984.

Colborne, Robert. *Fundamentals of Merchandise Presentation*. Cincinnati, Ohio: The Signs of Times Publishing Company, 1982.

Drucker, Peter F. *People and Performance*. New York: Harper & Row, Publishers, 1977.

Goldstein, E. Bruce. *Sensation and Perception*. Belmont, California: Wadsworth Publishing Company, 1989.

Hofer, Jack. *Total Sensuality*. New York: Grosset & Dunlap, 1978.

Mowen, John C. *Consumer Behavior*. New York: Macmillan Publishing Company, 1987.

Naisbitt, John. *Megatrends*. New York: Warner Books, Inc., 1982.

New York Times.

Novak, Adolph. *Store Planning & Design*. New York: Lebhar-Friedman Books, 1977.

Polanyi, Michael. *The Tacit Dimension*. Gloucester, Massachusetts: Peter Smith, 1983.

Rachlin, Howard. *Introduction to Modern Behaviorism*, Second edition. San Francisco: W.H. Freeman and Company, 1976.

Rowan, Roy. *The Intuitive Manager*. Boston, Toronto: Little, Brown and Company, 1986.

Rowe, Frank A. *Display Fundamentals*. Cincinnati, Ohio: Signs of the Times Publishing Company, 1979.

Schiffman, Leon G., and Leslie Lazar Kanuk. *Consumer Behavior*. Englewood Cliffs, New Jersey: Prentice-Hall, Inc., 1978.

_____. *International Trends in Retailing*. Chicago: Arthur Andersen & Co., Spring 1986 (Volume 3, No. 1).

_____. *Visual Merchandising*. New York: National Retail Merchants Association, 1976.

Photo Credits

Croscill, Pg 104: Mayo Studios, New York City.

Bergdorf Goodman, Pg 16: Design by Norwood Oliver Design Associates. Photo credit Mark Ross, Interior Design Magazine, January 1979.

All other photographs from author's files.

Acknowledgements

I would like to express my sincere appreciation to the many supportive clients who permitted a new methodology into their established systems. What seems easily acceptable today, was courageous then.

I am grateful to Joel Stein of McGraw-Hill for his steady guidance, and to my editor Vilma Barr who first saw the potential of a book in my approach.

To P.K. Anderson of Visual Merchandising/Store Planning who prodded patiently to open up the channels of writing for me. Her friendship and professionalism are unparalleled.

The following friends and colleagues encouraged and contributed to the formative and continuing stages of my career which led to the ideas and theories that eventually became my practices.

- Arline W. Gardner for her early foresight and dedication.
- Claudio Nazzari whose open, humorous, inventive spirit of teaching and giving gave me a new direction.
- Sid Diamond who has been my business godfather.
- George Homer Jr. who has helped with his comments and tech-assistance.
- Joe Rivers of Frederick Atkins Inc. Bob Carullo of Walker Group/CNI who have given advice on their areas of expertise.
- Dave Gandell of Creative Shopping Center Management, Joe Seigel of N.R.F., Charlotte Schluger of the I.C.S.C., Neal Tyler of Amcena, and Peck Klose of Frederick Atkins Inc. who put me and my ideas in front of their colleagues and clients.
- John Murphy, formerly of the N.R.M.A. who believed that retail audiences would enjoy and be educated by a unique approach.
- To Piergiorgio and Vittorio Coin, Carlos Rocca, Francis DeMoge, Graham White, Helen and Desmond Preston, Irving Ludmer for their support and acceptance.
- To Dorothy Pollock who always allowed good design and unique presentations to mix with fun and excitement.
- To Salvatore Marra of Alexanders, Roz Jacobs of C.P.I., John Ryder of McCurdys who shared their insights on blue light, good taste and turning right.
- To the Store Planners, Display Directors, Visual Merchants, Students of Design who have added the sparkle and personality to lifeless items.
- Gibbs Murray, my first designer and currently director of Display & Exhibits at F.I.T., for his talent and humor.
- To Elizabeth Jacobson who always made the most of every situation.
- To the members of N.A.D.I. for their constant efforts to improve the state of the art of store presentation.
- To Sandy Driesen who unselfishly copied, listened, and recopied mountains of material, and gave consistent encouragement.
- And lastly to the wonderful friends and co-workers who created museum quality masterpieces from foam board, tissue, wood, metal and plastic.
- To the memory of Rudy Stein whose incantation of the New Vision "Bible" put balance back into focus.
- And to my dearest friend, Tom Granfield, whose brilliance and generosity of spirit shall not soon come this way again.

Glossary

Add-on purchasing. The goal of most merchants is to extend the initial intent of shoppers by enticing purchases beyond the defined or impulse item. The add-on item is generally not advertized but its sale is encouraged by visual presentation.

Aesthetic distance. The scale of each object to be viewed must be in proportion to its surroundings in order to best obtain a specific reaction. The entry and passage to an object of art or merchandise is part of the viewers experience. Some of the most memorable pieces of art, such as Michelangelo's David in the Academia in Florence, or Monet's Water Lilies in the Museum of Modern Art in New York, are as dramatically placed as the Christmas tree in Rockerfeller Center.

Autonomic system. The instinctual parts of our responses that are not governed by rational decisions. Some are purely physical, and some have been built into our being by ages of selective breeding in response to physical phenomena.

Broken sizes. When items are bought for either RTW or home there can be a range of sizes that are selected by the store buyer that fit the historic profile of their clientele. A loss of one or more of the sizes within each specific style group is called broken sizing. This happens more often with fashion or seasonal items.

Category killer. Single product dominance, selection of all brands and some well priced house brands under one roof gave these free standing stores an enormous edge. However, their immediate success following their introduction, brought swift competition. Their birth, maturity, and eventual failure for many, was one of the fastest cycles of a retail type operation.

Check out. In the sense of product sales rather than a cash station, the term is buyer jargon for rate of sale.

Cladding. A construction of any material around a column or fronting for a surface to prepare it to accept merchandise.

Co-op funds. Manufacturer monies that are earmarked for advertising or for in-store presentation. The shift to the latter is pronounced.

Critical mass. An amount of merchandise in height, width and depth that increases the perception of product credibility.

Destination shopper. As implied, a person who sets out to buy a specific item and is not motivated by external impulse. They generally are out to purchase a non-glamorous item, but can be enticed to buy a second item. As an example, the fabric and notions department in malls and stores were eliminated because of their high cost and low return. Although 95 percent of their purchases were made by destination shoppers who shopped other areas, they were eliminated. From the moment that happened adjacent departments lost a healthy percentage of their sales. This literally drove these shoppers to fabric specialty stores.

Display (Display Director). This is now defined as the art of theatrical presentation where the merchandise shown is only for presentation. The items for sale are nearby. The term has unfortunately lost some of its elan to the more imposing, business-like, Visual Merchandise Director. However, the practitioners of "display" have extraordinary unique talent that should be valued as highly as the best advertising and promotion directors.

Drive aisles. Flexible pathways that lead from the main aisle to departmental locations that holds prime merchandise.

End of Series. Essentially a European term that is understood by customers to be badly broken, but still highly desirable best sellers. Many stores re-coordinate and identify the stock as such and even have a separate area on the sales floor that holds most of this stock. It is hardly ever marked-down, and definitely not clearance.

End-use function. This term comes into use more frequently in mass presentation, or when coordinated merchandise is regrouped. It refers to the assembly of stock by customer use, i.e. all bottoms - shorts, pants, skirts or all tops placed on one fixture, or in one location.

Etalagists. French word for display people. They worked in an area for presentation that was limited to a narrow shelf (etal) behind the show window.

Grid Pattern. A standard, but rather inane way, of placing fixtures on a plan. It virtually guarantees a difficult situation to make needed internal mid-season changes.

Highly saturated. Intense colors generally primary or secondary. Saturation refers to purity, unadulterated by other colors, black, or white which, would mute the base tone.

Hypermarche. This are primarily European phenomena. They are superstores sometimes over 200,000 square feet on one level holding all ranges of clothing, home, accessories, and a supermarket. So far they have not succeeded in the U.S., as supermarkets have only gained a small share of market in Europe.

In-Line Stores. This term is used by the shopping center industry to define those shops who have long-term leases. Rather than use the term specialty stores, it is applied to all stores that are not in the category of carts, kiosks, center court tables, or major anchors.

In-Store Marketing. The future of all presentation will be the use of all marketing information about product and customer to market merchandise rather than just make presentations.

Island department. Generally a space that does not have a wall backing. It can be used for sub-dividing a category, bridging two categories, or as a swing area.

Jobber. This almost extinct profession was also known as "middle-men." They would gather merchandise from many manufacturers to re-distribute to small retail outlets. Consolidations in retail and direct manufacturer to outlets has almost eliminated jobbers.

Mark-down. Frequently mis-used. The cycle of goods from arrival to sales is as generally follows:
- Goods arrive, the initial purchase price is then marked-on for the first selling price.
- The goods can be marked-down for special promotion or sales.
- They can then be marked-up and return to first price.
- A final mark-down is a clearance.

There are laws that govern the shifting of prices.

Merchandise specialist. A position that was started and extended by companies who needed a constant liaison between department managers and central office buyers. The specialist knew the merchandise and the market for each store and could place it within the cubic department space for a consistency of stock level and corporate presentation.

Package Buying (Program Buying). Manufacturers attempt to sell an entire line or series by giving inducements such as advertising monies, fixturing, co-op sales help. Most programs are good for both buyer and seller as the product presence is enhanced on the sales floor.

RTW (Ready-to-wear). The enormous amount of all clothing worn today fits this description. Before the ages of mechanization, almost all garments were made-to-measure. Men's, women's, and children's, clothing comprise the heart of retail sales.

Sales penetration. When customers enter a store the percent of those that make purchases form the number who have penetrated.

Sales service. A much used and mis-used term. Each store supplys some sales assistance even if it is only at the cash/wrap station. Most customers have been educated to do some self-selection and will browse on their own. In this respect, presentation is the first line of sales-service.

Schaufenstermacher. The German term that describes the entire function of designer, craftsman who created and constructed display. Today, German stores incorporate carpenters, painters, metalworkers, and electricians in the display department.

Secondary aisles. Like drive aisles, they are temporary passages that can shift as the assortment balance changes. They can define an area as well as lead to a focal point. Their width varies with their distance from the main entry and the depth of stock.

SKU (Stock Keeping Unit). For every different style, and each color within a style a separate SKU number is given. A change of size in RTW does not mean a new SKU. But in housewares, different size or capacity will have another number.

Stimulus Progression. Used by the Muzak Corporation, it is a highly sophisticated idea that uses the cycle of human emotions effected by the changing hourly physical ambient phenomena. Its goal is to produce moods that govern responses that are positively directed by the suggestions of the elements of sound. It is legal and it works. As hearing is only one of the five senses, imagine the power of this control with sight, smell, taste, and touch, using similar methodology.

Strip malls. These were the first out-of-center city shopping areas. They were built on one side of a parkway in a straight line. Facades and signs of individual shops faced the road. During the course of years they grew, waned, and became favorable again along with the growth and decline of covered regional malls, and population movement.

Swing area. A prime space from entry that holds seasonally hot items. The life of the merchandise desirability here should be about one month. This space is used to pull items from adjacent departments to use of items that coordinate with storewide promotions.

Triangulate. In seeing it refers to the ability of the eyes to pinpoint a place no matter what the distance. In presentation it refers to pyramiding of stock in three dimensions or using converging diagonals in two dimensions.

Vanilla box. Current usage is a store that has been vacated in a mall in preparation for the entry of a new, temporary or neophyte tenant. The term implies a banality which unfortunately cannot be rectified by untested retailers.

Visual merchants. During the early 1970's the term gained favor as the responsibility of the display director increased. The opportunity to assume new presence and financial policy making was given, and a few display staff emerged to create their mark by showing their administrative and fiscal talents. The term is now almost fully separated as one who is responsible for the bottom line of the company through artistic presentation.

Vitrinisti. Italian jargon endearingly used for anyone whose responsibility is visual. Formerly dealing only with window presentation, vitrinisti also handle the store interior.

Warehouse club. The newest form of retail and reputed to be the fastest growing percentage of market share. With an open policy of price mark-on and dealing with a paid membership of steadily employed, they grew in number through the 1980's. Pallet sales, concrete floors, bulk purchases, high quality merchandise, and low cost operations gave a price conscious public a new "smart shopping" experience. They were initiated by Sol Price, whose last name was fortuitous in naming the Price Club.

Index